the **low-carb gourmet**

the low-carb gourmet

RECIPES FOR THE NEW LIFESTYLE

Brigit Binns

photography by Valerie Martin

TEN SPEED PRESS
Berkeley | Toronto

TO CASEY, RONDA, AND LILY—MY CHERISHED SUPPORT TROUPE.

Copyright © 2004 by Brigit Binns
Photography © 2004 by Valerie Martin
Front cover photo by Valerie Martin

A Kirsty Melville Book

1⊜
Ten Speed Press
P.O. Box 7123
Berkeley, California 94707
www.tenspeed.com

Distributed in Australia by Simon and Schuster
Australia, in Canada by Ten Speed Press Canada,
in New Zealand by Southern Publishers Group,
in South Africa by Real Books, and in the United
Kingdom and Europe by Airlift Book Company.

Cover and text design by **Catherine Jacobes Design**
Food styling by **Andrea Luchich**
Food styling assistance by **Loraine Battle**
Prop styling by **Carol Hacker**
Thank you to Sur La Table for providing props.

Library of Congress Cataloging-in-Publication Data
on file with the publisher.

ISBN 1-58008-630-6

Printed in China
First printing, 2004

1 2 3 4 5 6 7 8 9 10 — 09 08 07 06 05 04

CONTENTS

Breakfast *and* Brunch

75 Roast Chicken, Chard, and Sun-Dried Tomato Frittata

76 Smoked Salmon, Whipped Cream Cheese, and Red Onion Brik

78 Chicken-Apple Sausage, Spinach, and Gruyère Soufflé

79 Apple and Raspberry Crêpes with Nutmeg and Crème Fraîche

80 Baby Greens and Pink Grapefruit on a Bed of Sunny-Side-Up Eggs

82 Shirred Eggs on a Bed of Spinach with Roasted Peppers

Fish *and* Shellfish

87 Pepper-Crusted Soft-Shell Crabs with Grapefruit Beurre Blanc

90 Dungeness Crab and Fennel Salad with Ginger-Curry Aïoli

92 Vietnamese Salad on Sushi-Grade Yellowtail

93 Seared Scallops and Caramelized Cauliflower Florets with Salsa Verde

96 Pan-Roasted Sea Bass with Truffle-Leek Nage Sauce

98 Crayfish Soufflé with Tarragon Sabayon

100 Salmon Burgers with Pinot Noir Glaze and Pancetta Chips

103 Hazelnut-Crusted Freshwater Trout with Preserved Lemon Relish

Poultry, Game, *and* Meat

108 Seared Duck Breast with Blood Orange–Veal Stock Reduction

109 Pan-Fried Chicken Breasts with Sage and Ham Butter

110 Wine-Braised Chicken Thighs with Green Olives and Herbs

112 Porcini-Stuffed Turkey Thigh

114 Rabbit with Saffron and Fennel Ragoût and Whole-Wheat Linguine

117 Seared Lamb Noisettes with Pea, Feta, and Mint Salad

118 Grilled Quail in Escabèche (Tomato-Vinegar) Sauce

121 Braised, Grilled, Wine-Dark Short Ribs

124 Carpaccio-Wrapped Butter Lettuce and Palm Hearts with Chimichurri Sauce

126 Smoked Bacon and Pork Tenderloin Skewers with Three-Citrus Mojo

The Cheese Course

132 Cabrales and Manchego with Celery Hearts and Pedro Jimenez

134 Epoisses and Roquefort with Walnuts and Marc de Bourgogne

135 Scamorza and Pecorino Romano with Dried Figs and Vin Santo

136 Kefalotyri Grilled in a Vine Leaf, and Mild Feta with Kalamata Olives and Retsina

Dessert

141 Fresh Figs on Sauternes Gelée with Mint Mascarpone

142 Star Anise Flan with Blackberries

145 Grilled Peaches with Honey Ricotta

146 Roasted Strawberries with Pomegranate-Beaujolais Granita

147 Fresh Ginger and Mint Granita with Almond and Green Cardamom Cookies

148 Flourless Chocolate Cake with Raspberry Sauce

150 BASICS

154 INDEX

ACKNOWLEDGMENTS

I would like to offer my heartfelt thanks to the following wonderful people:

Lorena Jones for her long-standing confidence in me.

Kirsty Melville, for seeing the world of possibilities, and for acting on her vision.

Carrie Rodrigues, for shepherding the manuscript through a painstaking yet personal process to approach perfection.

Joseph Regal, the ultimate patient and loveable agent, who has gone out on increasingly small limbs to make things happen for me.

Andrea DeWit, for giving graciously of her time and advice on several photo shoots, and for her—and her husband Michael's—willingness to follow my low-carb advice (by the way, you guys look great!).

Mary Donkersloot, for offering advice, a voice of balance, and for making sure I stayed responsible on issues of nutrition.

Kit and Linda (The Elvis), for help in navigating the twists and turns of "The Dark Side" (publicity), among other things.

And the professionals who created the physical reality of the book:

Valerie Martin, for her luscious photography, can-do attitude, and infectious grin.

Catherine Jacobes, for giving the book a gracious and lovely look, and for letting my personality shine through.

Andrea Luchich, Lorraine Battle, and Carol Hacker, for creating food and ambiance that really do look good enough to eat.

Rebecca Pepper, for her smarts and incredible copyediting expertise, which forced me to answer questions I would have preferred to avoid.

And Joachim Splichal, Hans Rockenwagner, Evan Kleiman, Jody Maroni, Jean-François Méteigner, Marilyn Lewis, Joe Miller, and Tony Tammero, for personally teaching me so many, many things about food, and for turning me into a gourmet.

A trend is taking hold in this country that's becoming a movement, and there's not even a glimmer of a sign that it will ever fall from grace. Diets come and go with alarming rapidity, but especially after being embraced by doctors and many nutritionists, the low-carb phenomenon appears to be here to stay. Even chain restaurants are introducing low-carb choices, and in corporate America it takes a lot to shift a multimillion-dollar operation. (Many of these establishments are just now adding low-fat selections.)

But let's not look at the low-carb movement as a "diet." I'm offended by such terms, and ever since the Grapefruit Juice Diet gave me an ulcer in my early twenties, I've avoided them all. I call it a lifestyle choice, and it has served me well. Over the last three or four years, I have eaten fewer carbohydrates and more protein and green vegetables. I weigh the same as I did in my first year of college, and because I've seen what happens when I temporarily abandon the low-carb regimen for a week of pasta and bread (in Italy it's de rigueur, isn't it?), I know that over the long term, this is how I am going to continue to eat, and live.

In the true and final reckoning, eating and living well—luxuriously, with plenty of variation and excitement, and taking full advantage of good wines and the ethnic cuisines of the world—is probably more important to me than staying slim.

I'd like to say that I'm concerned about my health and longevity, but in actual fact vanity is more of a motivation than anything else. When I look good, I feel good, and strictly limiting carbs makes me look good. That's what I call realistic, healthy thinking. There's no doubt that limiting carbohydrate intake will cause almost everyone to lose weight, and lose it fast, so why doesn't everyone stick religiously to the lifestyle? Anyone who says they get bored with hard-boiled eggs and steak needs a little gentle education.

Vegetables and fish are the stars of this cuisine, and a free hand with spices, herbs, most condiments, fantastic vinegars, and luscious olive and nut oils means that the potential menu is almost limitless. Garlic, capers, lemons, anchovies, wasabi, curry, lemon grass, parsley—the pantry is full and very tasty. Yes, eggs are an important component of the lifestyle, but I ask you, what is boring about a soufflé? (I can scarcely bring myself to write the two words in the same sentence.) Low-carbohydrate gurus don't all agree with including grains, but it's becoming clear that for continued good health, reliance on fatty meats just doesn't make sense. That's why the Stellar Sides chapter in this book is longer than all the others and the Meat chapter is shorter: the goal should be lots of vegetables, salads, fish, and chicken and a little meat—lean and really satisfying—a bit of cheese, and a few whole grains. It's the way of the future.

In the true and final reckoning, eating and living well—luxuriously, with plenty of variation and excitement, and taking full advantage of good wines and the ethnic cuisines of the world—is probably more important to me than staying slim. That's why I've stayed away from diets all my life. But in this lifestyle, I can have my cake (as it were) and eat it too. I can eat well, live well, feel good, and, as a result, look great. It's what I've cared about and pursued all my life, and I wouldn't dream of stopping now.

A Life Well Lived

I spent my childhood in the Southern California of the early seventies, a simple and bucolic time of cheese soufflés, green and fence-less front lawns, and unlimited parking. We dug up mussels on beaches north of Santa Barbara and consumed them with-

in the hour—bright, almost fluorescent orange inside their somber shells, simply steamed and gobbled with melted butter. Halfway through my college career I spent a year in Malaysia, Hong Kong, and Taiwan. I roamed the street stalls and narrow lanes, watching the true masters as they would—with only a few deft movements—create a steaming bowl of tripe soup piled with bright, glistening greens, or a shockingly fresh, tender fish submerged and poached in a subtle aromatic broth. After graduation and a sybaritic, eye-opening summer in Greece, I lived—for reasons of economy—a few blocks from New York City's Chinatown, where I continued to roam and taste, widening my culinary and cultural horizons in the ultimate melting pot. Suddenly, an affair of the heart caused a move to England, where I was to remain for more than five years.

During my years in England, the best times were the weekends and vacations in Greece, Italy, and France: the restaurant just outside Genoa, where the tenderest pasta I'd ever eaten was napped with a bright green sauce that was pesto but was some-how *more* like pesto than any I'd had before...the Lyon eatery where I thought a phrase on the menu translated as "All our frog's legs come in the door under their own power"...the little seaside shack on the Costa Smerelda of Sardinia, where live lob-sters were grilled and served with a sauce made from mounds of chopped parsley, anchovies, vinegar, and fruity olive oil. In Greece, there was no Michelin guide nor any need of one—my eyes and nose were the best guides (and my willingness to take a road for no other reason than that it looked smaller on the map than all the others). Then, in the winter of 1989, I unexpectedly moved from England to Spain's southern coast, the Costa del Sol. After six years of London's cold, wet winters I was like a child at Christmas, being given the gift I wanted most in all the world.

I'll never forget the moment I first set eyes on the house, as I pulled over the top of the hill in a big, ungainly truck filled with furniture. The sea sparkled incred-ibly blue against the dun brown hillside, and the freshly whitewashed walls stood out starkly against the scrubby land. And the garden. The lemon tree was already heavy with fruit, and the fig tree bore hundreds of pear-shaped knobs that spoke of luscious, plump black fruits to come.

Nasturtiums of several different hues trailed down the retaining wall and threatened to invade the brick and iron barbecue that was tucked into that sheltered corner. I made the woody, perennial herbs like rosemary, sage, marjoram, oregano, and lemon thyme into ornamental features, planting them around the rest of the garden, next to the verbena or in front of a wide bank of oleander. As for regular thyme, the entire hill behind the house was covered with it, growing wild. Wiggy, my Staffordshire terrier, loved to snarfle and root around on that hillside, and she always brought in the wonderful perfume, like a cloud of scent following an elegant woman. She was re-christened "Wild-Thyme Wiggy."

The house and garden were perfect for entertaining, and I soon fell into a habit of small, frequent get-togethers. In the summer, the rustic barbecue next to the kitchen garden was the focus, and in the winter it was the big stone fireplace. Not using chemicals in the garden meant that a salad could be gathered only moments before serving. To avoid any activity during the heat of the day, I marinated swordfish or pork for the brochettes early in the morning. Once, after a trip to Greece, I decided to try flaming a fish with ouzo on a bed of oregano branches. It was only after my singed eyebrows grew back that I perfected the recipe, using a lot less ouzo and fresh (not dried) oregano branches, and standing well away from the platter.

I was quite happy being a citizen of Europe, and my return to California twenty years after leaving was another unexpected turn in the road. But I've discovered many home-truths in the years since then, and I wouldn't want to live anywhere else. Current events (the first Gulf War), financial uncertainty, and romantic ups and downs aside, it's hard to deny that my day-to-day existence in Spain was pretty idyllic. Now that the days are filled with phone calls, faxes, e-mail, and crises, those years seem surrounded by a rosy hue. I'll never lose the perspective gained from ten years in Europe: it informs my every decision, every day. There was something peaceful, practical, and lyrical about that slowed-down attitude toward the world. It takes only a moment to remind yourself of the really important things in life, and high amongst them are good health and great spirit. I now know that it's how you feel, not where you are or how much you have, that makes life truly good.

The Low-Carb Life

In England, particularly after attending a professional, haute French–style cooking school, my menus were centered around butter, flour, and cream. By the time I moved to Spain, I was ready to lighten up my kitchen—I needed to lose 15 extra pounds if I was to don a bathing suit as constant attire. My love of vegetables and herbs, a certain need for economy, and my weight concerns led me to cook in a way that was new to me, but is still—with a few adjustments—the way I cook today, almost fifteen years later and twelve years after my return to America. I cooked from my garden, from the central vegetable and fish markets on the coast, and from a European pantry that included mustards, capers, anchovies, lentils, chickpeas, rice, saffron, pine nuts, superb olive oil, and all the wonderful wines of the region. I was successful in my attempt to shed fifteen pounds in the first six months after moving to Spain, but I always shied away from anything that could be labeled "healthy" cooking. About 4 years ago, an age-related slowing of the metabolism made it hard to maintain the weight I had come to expect and enjoy. That's when I started to cut down on refined flour, pasta, sugar, legumes, bread, and potatoes. The results were almost instantaneous, and I wouldn't give up my present physique or way of life for all the gold at the end of the rainbow.

I have never found the low-carb regime to be limiting or in any way boring. Over the years, the availability of fine and varied ingredients has become not just inspiring, but awesome. Every major city now has supermarkets that cater to concerned, serious cooks. The farmers' markets springing up everywhere bring the joy of chatty, choosy marketing to more and more people. For those who live far from a city, countless Internet companies offer quick, safe, and fairly reasonable delivery of global exotica, even perishable foods. It's easy to cook as though you live almost anywhere in the world now, whether the view out your window is of Kalamazoo, Long Island, or Eureka.

The food in this book is a hybrid—simple, low-carbohydrate dishes from all the places I've lived in, visited, and loved—France, Italy, Spain, Greece, China—as well as those I've loved without visiting: Japan, Vietnam, Latin America, and India. I would never call this type of food trendy, but it's often sensational and almost always practical. Best of all, it all adheres to a low-carbohydrate regimen that, if you follow it with enthusiasm and a sense of purpose, will provide you with a slim and ageless physique and the confidence to go forward into the next phase of your ever-stimulating life.

Atkins Is Dangerous?

You may have seen news stories decrying the Atkins diet. Keep this in mind: All Atkins is low-carb, but not all low-carb is Atkins.

In fact, if taken at face value the Atkins diet recommends a ludicrous amount of meat and fat. I predict that, eventually, strict adherence to the Atkins regime will fall from favor, and a more balanced low-carb approach like South Beach—which downplays fatty protein and allows some whole grains—will replace it. In practice, the best approach is something like a loose interpretation of the Zone diet: two handfuls of green beans, a handful of lean protein, and a tablespoon of olive oil. But that won't sell a million books.

At the end of the day—literally—it's the total calorie count that matters, and calories derived from protein (and some fat) satisfy more than calories from carbohydrates, so less are consumed. Try this experiment: One day, at 11 A.M. on an empty stomach, eat a hard-boiled egg (2 ounces). The next day at 11 A.M. on a similarly empty stomach, eat 2 ounces of potato chips. Which makes you feel fuller?

Members of the nutrition community have long had their undies in a bundle because study after study has shown that low-carb diets do not cause heart or kidney disease, nor do they raise cholesterol. Many of them came out against low-carb diets in the beginning and have found themselves having to eat crow. So if a few isolated

cases come along that—anecdotally—blame Atkins for heart disease, they are going to embrace the reports and resurrect their cause. But a sensible low-carb regime—not vast quantities of bacon, cheese, and steak, but spinach, chicken, olive oil, and a little butter—works. And it works well. People have lost weight and kept it off, and stayed healthy in the thirty-one years since Atkins published his first book. And weight loss is very near and dear to the hearts of Americans.

Like most food regimes, the Atkins approach needs tweaking. That is why, in this book, I emphasize that low-carb is not a license to gorge on protein. Simply put, the problem is that people don't know what else to eat. I've tried to address that dilemma here, showing a healthy, satisfying approach that emphasizes vegetables and heart-healthy fats, lean protein and eggs, and plenty of exercise.

Appetizers *and* Small Bites

If you are accustomed to snacking between meals on potato or tortilla chips, crackers, or breadsticks, you will have to adjust your mindset.

TO WHET THE APPETITE for the meal to come, we serve appetizers. They must seduce the eye as well as the palate, awaken and tease the taste buds, and set the scene for the ensuing repast. We want appetizers to complement the main course but never overwhelm it. These are some of the same rules that apply to conventional menu planning; however, the low-carb menu planner has a few other things to keep in mind. If you intend to serve hungry diners a light main course of fish or poultry, assorted vegetables, and a pretty—but really just a token—dessert, it's important to make sure they don't leave the table hungry. One way to fill up the void is to serve a substantial appetizer that is also low in carbohydrates, like Roasted Eggplant and Ricotta Rolatini with Fresh Tomato Sauce (page 12), or Lamb Sausage Dolmades (page 16). Since you will not be offering crackers and cheese, chips, or breadsticks, you may want to provide a stand-up appetizer as well, something you can snack on while chatting in the kitchen, like Haricots Frites with Tarragon Sauce (page 25), Caviar-Topped Deviled Eggs (page 18), Tuna Tartare on Jicama Rounds (page 21), or Dried Fig and Cognac Tapenade (page 13).

If you are accustomed to snacking between meals on potato or tortilla chips, crackers, or breadsticks, you will have to adjust your mindset. Cheese and salami are not the answer either (both are fine in moderation only, not as a constant, daily snack). Atkins and other low-carb food companies market crackers and bread, but you will probably find their flavor and texture somewhat lacking. In my book, it's best to stick to snacks that are naturally low in carbohydrates, not ones that are that way through some unnatural, contrived twist. Nuts contain beneficial oils and fats and make a good snack, as do Wasa light rye crackers—probably the only widely available cracker with only 7 grams of carbohydrates per 8-gram cracker—served with a bit of interesting cheese. Crudités are always a good choice (keep carrots to a minimum), and you can make creamy, rich dips with impunity. Choose from guacamole, garlic-chive, and eggplant "caviar" (skip the hummus because of the high carb count of chickpeas). While not especially elegant, pork rinds are satisfyingly crunchy and make a fine base for light, sour cream–based spreads and dips. Smoked salmon and cream cheese can be processed with chives and few drops of lemon juice. In every case, it is better to make your own rather than purchase prepared concoctions that are often full of extenders and chemical additives. When making dips and spreads, avoid low-fat dairy products, because they are higher in carbohydrates.

Once in a while, take advantage of this unorthodox canapé base: Place a paper towel on a plate and spread a single layer of thinly sliced salami on top, then cover with another paper towel. Crisp in the microwave for 1 minute, then peel off the paper towel. The resulting salami "chips" will have many tiny holes where the fat has melted out onto the paper towel; you'll be left with a tasty base for fresh and light mixtures like whole-milk ricotta, diced tomatoes, or curried sour cream. Another not exactly "gourmet" snack is celery sticks stuffed with whipped cream cheese (not the light version) and topped with a mixture of chopped olives and finely chopped green onions.

For an elemental, back-to-the womb kitchen snack, make the homemade ricotta on page 48 and, while it is still warm, serve a few spoonfuls on small plates with a drizzle of the best extra virgin olive oil you can afford—preferably a green, Tuscan oil—and 3 or 4 grains only of fleur de sel. This is serious, unabashed manna from heaven for a true gourmet (in my humble opinion). If you like smoky flavors, scatter with just a few grains of smoked salt. It sounds odd, but it's delicious as long as you really do use only a few grains.

Roasted Eggplant *and* Ricotta Rolatini *with* Tomato Sauce

SERVES 6 * When I worked as a caterer in southern Spain, this was one of my standards—appealing equally to the many Brits, Germans, Danes, and Americans who rounded out the sun-kissed expatriate population. You can make the tomato sauce a day ahead (omitting the basil) and refrigerate it; warm it through just before serving, and then stir in the basil. Look for straight, not curved eggplants for this dish, and be sure to use whole-milk ricotta (or make your own; see page 48).

TOMATO SAUCE

1 tablespoon olive oil

1 clove garlic, smashed with the side of a large, heavy knife

1 (28-ounce) can peeled Italian plum tomatoes, with their juice

$^1/_4$ cup dry white wine or vermouth

$^1/_2$ teaspoon fine sea salt

Freshly ground black pepper

2 tablespoons julienned fresh basil leaves, loosely packed

Extra virgin olive oil, for brushing

3 small Japanese eggplants, 5 to 6 ounces each

Fine sea salt and freshly ground black pepper

1 cup (8 ounces) whole-milk ricotta

$^1/_3$ cup freshly grated Parmigiano-Reggiano or grana padano cheese

1$^1/_2$ teaspoons finely chopped flat-leaf parsley

$^1/_8$ teaspoon ground nutmeg, preferably freshly grated

1 large egg yolk

To prepare the tomato sauce, place a large sauté pan over medium-low heat, and add the olive oil. Add the garlic and cook, stirring, for about 2 minutes, or until golden (do not allow it to burn). Add the tomatoes and their juice, crushing the tomatoes thoroughly with your hand (cut away the cores if they are tough), and increase the heat to medium-high. Stir together and bring to a boil, then adjust the heat so that the sauce simmers briskly, uncovered. Add the wine, salt, and pepper. Simmer for 15 minutes, breaking up the tomato chunks with a wooden spoon. Remove from the heat and stir in the basil. (Remove the garlic just before serving.)

Preheat the oven to 425°F. Brush 2 baking sheets with olive oil. Cut off the stems and bases of the eggplants and slice them lengthwise about $^1/_4$ inch thick. Place on the baking sheets, brush the tops lightly with olive oil, and season lightly with salt and pepper. Bake until softened and golden, about 10 minutes. Set aside.

Reduce the oven heat to 375°F. In a bowl, combine and whisk together with a fork the ricotta, Parmigiano-Reggiano, parsley, nutmeg, egg yolk, salt, and a generous grinding of black pepper.

Brush the base of a ceramic baking dish lightly with olive oil. Place a generous teaspoon of the filling mixture at the wider end of each eggplant slice and roll up. Stand the rolls on their ends in the baking dish, nestling them together to keep the ends from unrolling. Spoon about $^1/_3$ cup of the tomato sauce around the edges, and cover with aluminum foil. Bake for 10 minutes, then let stand for 5 minutes before serving. Place 3 rolatini on each plate, with a few dollops of tomato sauce around the edges.

173 calories, 8 grams net carbs (10 grams less 2 grams fiber), 11 grams fat (5 grams saturated)

Dried Fig and Cognac Tapenade

MAKES ABOUT 1 CUP, SERVING 8 (CAN BE HALVED OR DOUBLED) * I've had a love affair with figs since I lived in Spain. I used to pick the luscious fruit straight from the tree just outside the window of the dining room—if I got to it before the birds. The problem with figs is that they are not worth picking or eating until they are soft and slightly split, and of course the birds know this too. Ripe or dried, I was loath to give up figs after starting the low-carb regimen. Thankfully, the high fiber content helps to erase the carbohydrates usually present in fresh and dried fruits.

2 salt-packed or oil-packed anchovy fillets, rinsed with warm water and patted dry

2 cloves garlic, thinly sliced

1 teaspoon minced or grated lemon zest

5 ounces mild green olives, such as picholine or lucques (about ³/₄ cup), pitted

4 ounces brine-cured black olives, such as niçoise (about ²/₃ cup), pitted

2 dried brown figs, stemmed and thinly sliced

¹/₄ teaspoon minced fresh rosemary

1 tablespoon extra virgin olive oil

2 teaspoons Cognac or brandy

Celery sticks and wedges of jicama, for serving

Using a mortar and pestle, pound the anchovy, garlic, and lemon zest into a smooth paste. In a food processor, purée the olives and figs until smooth. If your mortar is large enough, add the puréed olive mixture, rosemary, olive oil, and Cognac to the garlic paste in it. Stir until smooth and season to taste. (Or whisk everything together in a bowl.) Cover and refrigerate for at least 2 hours, to allow the flavors to marry. It will keep for up to 1 week. Serve in a ramekin in the center of a platter, surrounded by celery sticks and jicama wedges. Provide a small cocktail knife for serving.

99 calories, 5 grams net carbs (6 grams less 1 gram fiber), 8 grams fat (1 gram saturated)

Prime Beef Tataki *with* Ponzu Sauce

SERVES 10 * Tataki is a popular Japanese dish most often made with super-fresh ahi tuna. This unabashedly luxurious version is almost like an Asian-accented carpaccio, but the beef is sliced far thicker than for carpaccio. The slices of cool, rosy-red beef look most delectable on a buffet.

2 pounds whole, trimmed USDA Prime beef tenderloin (fillet), very cold

1 tablespoon vegetable oil

2 tablespoons sweet soy sauce (available at Asian markets or substitute dark soy sauce)

About ¹/₄ teaspoon freshly ground black pepper

MARINADE

¹/₃ cup tamari or low-sodium soy sauce

¹/₄ cup mirin (sweet Japanese cooking wine) or sherry

3 green onions, white and light green parts only, thinly sliced

2 large cloves garlic, thinly sliced

Zest of 1 lemon, coarsely grated

PONZU SAUCE

4 tablespoons low-sodium soy sauce

2 tablespoons rice vinegar

1¹/₂ tablespoons granular Splenda

1 tablespoon fresh lemon juice

1 tablespoon fresh lime juice

1 teaspoon ginger juice (or ginger paste; see note on page 21)

2 tablespoons finely snipped chives

About 2 cups fresh alfalfa sprouts, for serving

Preheat the oven to 500°F for a good 30 minutes to be sure it is nice and hot. Rub all sides of the beef with the vegetable oil, then rub in the sweet soy sauce and season with the pepper. Place on a rack over a roasting pan and sear in the hot oven for 15 minutes. The internal temperature, in the very center, should be 115°F. Immediately transfer the roasting rack to a tray (to catch the juices; do not keep over the roasting pan or the beef will continue to cook). Set in a cool place to stop the cooking as quickly as possible.

To prepare the marinade, in a heavy-duty resealable plastic bag large enough to hold the beef, combine the tamari, mirin, green onions, garlic, and lemon zest. As soon as the beef is cool enough to handle, transfer it to the bag and refrigerate for at least 6 hours, and up to 24 hours, turning over occasionally.

About 45 minutes before you plan to serve, place the bag in the freezer (this will firm the beef and make it easier to cut even slices). After 25 minutes, remove the beef from the bag and discard the marinade.

To make the Ponzu sauce, in a bowl whisk together the soy sauce, vinegar, Splenda, lemon and lime juice, ginger juice, and chives.

Slice the beef crosswise with a very sharp knife into ¹/₄-inch-thick slices, keeping them to an even thickness if possible. Fan the slices, overlapping, on a large platter and let stand for 10 minutes to take the chill off the meat. Surround with a lacy cordon of alfalfa sprouts, drizzle with the ponzu sauce, and serve.

228 calories, 2¹/₂ grams net carbs (3 grams less ¹/₂ gram fiber), 11 grams fat (4 grams saturated)

Lamb Sausage Dolmades

MAKES 12 DOLMADES, SERVING 4 (CAN BE DOUBLED) * Merguez is a unique, spicy Moroccan sausage with a rich, earthy flavor and a deep, red-brown color. It is fresh—not cooked or cured—and is usually available in well-stocked gourmet markets. If you must substitute another, milder lamb sausage, amp up the seasonings with paprika—preferably smoked paprika—and dark chile powder. Here, diced celery replaces the traditional rice, and a little crème fraîche serves to bind the mixture, which otherwise would be too crumbly.

1 (8-ounce) jar brine-packed grape leaves

8 ounces fresh lamb sausage, preferably Moroccan merguez, casings removed

$^{1}/_{4}$ cup water

2 stalks celery, ends trimmed, cut into $^{1}/_{4}$-inch dice

1 tablespoon pine nuts, toasted and finely chopped

$^{1}/_{2}$ teaspoon minced or grated lemon zest

3 tablespoons coarsely chopped flat-leaf parsley

2 tablespoons finely chopped fresh mint

$^{1}/_{4}$ teaspoon fine sea salt

Freshly ground black pepper

2 tablespoons crème fraîche or sour cream (full-fat)

1 tablespoon olive oil

$^{1}/_{2}$ cup homemade chicken broth, canned low-sodium chicken broth, or beef consommé

Pour the brine from the jar of grape leaves into a large bowl and ease out the folded leaves. Carefully remove 12 large leaves and return the brine and all the remaining leaves to the original jar. Save for another use (see page 136 for grilled, vine-leaf-wrapped cheese). Place the grape leaves in the bowl, cover with cold water, and separate them carefully. Let stand for 30 minutes.

While the leaves are soaking, place a large, nonstick or cast-iron skillet over medium heat. Add the sausage meat and $^{1}/_{4}$ cup water and cook, crumbling, mashing, and separating the meat with a wooden spoon into small pieces, until only just cooked through, about 5 minutes. Reduce the heat to low, add the celery, and cook for 2 minutes, to soften slightly. Remove the pan from the heat and stir in the pine nuts, lemon zest, parsley, mint, salt, a few turns of the peppermill, and the crème fraîche. Mix together thoroughly.

Trim the tough stems from the grape leaves and place one with the veined side up on a work surface, stem end closest to you. Overlap the bottom two sides of the leaf, if necessary, to make a solid surface for the filling. Scoop up 1 compact, rounded tablespoon of the filling and place it about $^{1}/_{2}$ inch above the bottom edge of the leaf. Fold the stem end up and over the filling, then fold in the two sides over the filling and roll up the packet tightly, starting at the bottom. Place seam side down in the base of a sauté pan or skillet just large enough to hold the packets snugly, and continue making packets until you have used all the filling. (If desired, cover and refrigerate the packets for up to 1 day before warming and serving.)

SAUCE

1 cup plain yogurt, preferably
European or Greek style

1 tablespoon finely chopped
fresh mint

1 clove garlic, minced or pressed

¼ teaspoon fine sea salt

Freshly ground black pepper

Lemon wedges, for serving

Drizzle the oil and the chicken broth over the dolmades. Over low heat, bring the liquid to a gentle simmer and cover the pan. Simmer for about 30 minutes, or until almost all of the liquid is absorbed. Uncover the pan and cool to room temperature.

To prepare the sauce, in a small, decorative bowl, whisk together the yogurt, mint, garlic, salt, and a generous grinding of pepper.

Serve the dolmades on a large platter, with the sauce and lemon wedges. Have paper napkins available. (Or refrigerate for up to 1 day and serve cold or at room temperature.)

315 calories, 7 grams net carbs (8 grams less 1 gram fiber), 20 grams fat (7 grams saturated)

Caviar-Topped Deviled Eggs

MAKES 16, SERVING 4 (CAN BE DOUBLED) ∗ Eggs, of course, are ubiquitous to the low-carb way of life, and the challenge is to find as many different ways of preparing them as possible. Deviled eggs have been popular off and on for generations. I like to top them with a tricolored mound of caviar, to make this version as elegant as it is addictive. Since the ravages to the sturgeon of the Caspian Sea have become known, a surprising number of new sturgeon and other fish roes have come onto the market. Both American and French sturgeon roe are of truly superior flavor and quality, and they are a far more environmentally sound choice. Paddlefish roe, salmon roe, and bright green, peppery wasabi "caviar" are other pleasing, eye-catching, and far less expensive possibilities.

8 very fresh extra-large eggs

2¹/₂ tablespoons Aïoli-Mayo Base (page 150) or store-bought mayonnaise

¹/₂ teaspoon Dijon mustard

³/₄ teaspoon white wine vinegar

1¹/₂ tablespoons drained capers

Scant 1 tablespoon finely chopped flat-leaf parsley

1 olive oil–or salt-packed anchovy fillet (salt-packed anchovies must be halved lengthwise into 2 fillets; use only 1)

¹/₄ teaspoon fine sea salt, plus more to taste

White pepper, preferably freshly ground

¹/₄ cup caviar of your choice, or 4 teaspoons each wasabi caviar, tobiko caviar or salmon roe, and domestic paddlefish or golden whitefish caviar

Carefully place the eggs in a wide, deep saucepan and add cold water to cover. Place over medium heat and bring to a boil. As soon as the water begins to boil, remove the pan from the heat, cover, and let stand for 11 minutes. Transfer the eggs to a bowl of ice water and let stand for 5 to 10 minutes. Strike each egg against the side of the bowl to crack the shell slightly. If desired, peel immediately, or let stand in the water for up to 1 hour (the eggs will be easier to peel if allowed to stand in the water after you crack the shells).

Peel the eggs, halve them lengthwise, and scoop the yolks out into a food processor. Reserve the whites, cut side down, in a single layer to prevent splitting. (The whites can be refrigerated, loosely covered with a towel, for up to 2 hours before filling.)

Add the aïoli-mayo base, mustard, vinegar, capers, parsley, anchovy, salt, and a tiny pinch of pepper to the food processor. Pulse to combine, scraping down the sides of the bowl as necessary. Taste and adjust the seasoning. (The mixture can be refrigerated for up to 2 hours before filling the egg whites.)

About 15 minutes before serving, scoop the mixture into the egg white halves, packing it in densely (leave a fairly flat top, ready for the caviar). Arrange the stuffed eggs on a platter and use two demitasse spoons to place about ³/₄ teaspoon of one caviar, or ¹/₄ teaspoon of each of three caviars, atop each egg (using one spoon to scoop, the other to push the caviar off the spoon and into position). Serve at once.

273 calories, 2 grams net carbs (2¹/₂ grams less ¹/₂ gram fiber), 21 grams fat (5 grams saturated)

Oyster-Wasabi Shots

SERVES 6 ∗ I have to warn you: this recipe is not for the faint of heart! When I tested these sinus-clearing, peppery apéritifs on a group of well-traveled, food-loving (and trusting) friends, one of the guests uttered a shout and started jumping up and down in what we all thought was grave distress. Oh dear, I thought to myself. But after a moment of reckoning, he said, "What the hell was that?! I love it!" And beware the humble, unassuming oyster; somewhat counterintuitively, each oyster contains about 1^1/$_2$ grams of carbohydrates—not an issue in this dish, but problematic if you have more than six at a time.

3 ounces aquavit

6 small, fresh oysters such as Olympias, freshly shucked (or use preshucked Chesapeake or Pacific oysters)

^{3}/$_4$ teaspoon prepared wasabi paste, or to taste

1^1/$_2$ teaspoons domestic or imported black caviar, tobiko, or salmon roe caviar

^{3}/$_4$ teaspoon very finely chopped fresh cilantro

1 teaspoon grated or minced orange zest

Place the aquavit in the freezer for at least 2 hours before you plan to serve. Chill 6 shot glasses, preferably the straight-sided variety.

If using the very large, shucked Pacific oysters, cut them into halves or quarters. Working quickly, place 1 tablespoon of aquavit into each of the chilled glasses and top with ^{1}/$_8$ teaspoon of wasabi paste, or to taste. Top with an oyster, and top each oyster with ^{1}/$_4$ teaspoon caviar and a tiny pinch each of cilantro and orange zest. Serve immediately.

If it is possible to do so graciously, drink the whole thing in one gulp.

79 calories, 2 grams net carbs (2 grams less 0 grams fiber), 2 grams fat (^{1}/$_2$ gram saturated)

Tuna Tartare *on* Jicama Rounds

SERVES 6 * Lemon grass adds a bright, clean, and citrusy perfume to the ever-popular, stylish, and low-carb-friendly tuna tartare. The earthy tamari balances the high notes and makes these cool, crunchy little bites unexpectedly satisfying.

DRESSING

1 large egg yolk

1^1/$_2$ tablespoons tamari or low-sodium soy sauce

^{3}/$_4$ teaspoon grated fresh ginger, with the juices (or ginger paste; see Note)

1 teaspoon extra-strong (imported) Dijon mustard

1 teaspoon granular Splenda

^{1}/$_4$ cup seasoned rice vinegar

^{1}/$_3$ cup peanut oil

1 tablespoon toasted sesame oil

1^1/$_2$ to 2 pounds jicama, refrigerated until just before serving

^{3}/$_4$ pound best-quality ahi tuna, cut into ^{1}/$_8$-inch dice with a very sharp knife

2 medium shallots, finely chopped

3 tablespoons finely chopped tender inner hearts of lemon grass (about 2 thick stalks)

^{1}/$_2$ teaspoon fine sea salt

^{1}/$_2$ teaspoon freshly ground black pepper

Finely snipped chives and/or sliced green onion, for garnish

To prepare the dressing, in a food processor, combine the egg yolk, tamari, ginger, mustard, and Splenda and process until smooth, scraping down the sides of the bowl as necessary. Add the vinegar and process for a few seconds, then, with the motor running, drizzle in the peanut and sesame oils, processing until the mixture is thick and creamy. Keep refrigerated until just before serving, for up to 2 days if desired.

Chill a large, flat serving platter.

Slice the jicama ^{1}/$_4$ inch thick. Using a 2-inch cookie cutter, cut as many rounds of jicama as possible, and place on the chilled serving platter. In a medium bowl, toss together the tuna, shallots, lemon grass, salt, and pepper. Stir in enough of the tamari dressing to coat—but not soak—the mixture. (The tuna should be served immediately, but if necessary you could cover and refrigerate it for up to 30 minutes.)

Spoon a generous teaspoon of the very cold tartare on top of each jicama round. Scatter with a few chives and/or green onions, and serve immediately.

NOTE: Japanese supermarkets and websites carry tubes of ginger paste, which are indispensable for the busy cook. After you've opened it, the paste will last for several months in the refrigerator, and it tastes exactly like grated fresh ginger.

267 calories, 6 grams net carbs (12 grams less 6 grams fiber), 16 grams fat (3 grams saturated)

Sliced Mushrooms *with* Calvados-Cured Salmon Gravlax

SERVES 6 TO 8 * I love this gutsy California-style update of a refined Roger Verge dish. Freeze any remaining salmon in 4-ounce portions; one or two can be quickly thawed for impromptu hors d'oeuvres, and the texture of the salmon does not suffer from freezing. (It's great in dips and spreads, scrambled eggs, and to top the occasional pizza.) Splenda tends to clump as soon as it gets damp, so be sure to sprinkle it evenly rather than mixing it with the other curing ingredients, as you would with sugar.

1 small white onion, coarsely chopped

1 small leek, white and light green parts only, well washed and coarsely chopped

2 cups fresh flat-leaf parsley sprigs, coarsely chopped

2 cups fresh tarragon sprigs, coarsely chopped

1 small bunch chives, coarsely chopped

1 tablespoon domestic Dijon mustard

$^1/_2$ teaspoon ground allspice

$^1/_2$ teaspoon ground nutmeg

2$^1/_2$ tablespoons coarse sea salt

$^1/_4$ cup Calvados (French apple brandy; do not substitute apple schnapps)

1 small side wild salmon (about 1$^1/_2$ pounds), picked over for bones

1 tablespoon granular Splenda

Three days before you plan to serve the dish, in a food processor, combine the onion, leek, parsley, tarragon, and chives and process into a rough paste. Transfer the mixture to a mixing bowl and add the mustard, spices, salt, and Calvados. Mix together well.

On a large work surface, lay a 3-foot-long piece of plastic wrap and spread half of the curing paste down the center in a flat, wide strip, keeping it at least 2 inches away from all the edges. Lay the salmon, skin side down, over the paste. Spread the remaining paste over the flesh side of the salmon, and sprinkle evenly with the Splenda. Fold the edges of the wrap in, and then lay another 3-foot piece of plastic wrap over the top, tucking the edges of the top piece underneath to make an airtight seal. Place the wrapped salmon in a large roasting pan to catch any leakage and refrigerate for at least 3 days, turning it over every 8 to 12 hours (the salmon will keep this way for up to 1 week and the flavor will only improve).

PISTACHIO OIL VINAIGRETTE

1¹/₂ tablespoons domestic Dijon mustard

2 tablespoons white wine vinegar

1 teaspoon fresh lemon juice

1 tablespoon pistachio or hazelnut oil

2 tablespoons mild extra virgin olive oil

2 tablespoons fresh tarragon leaves

Scant ¹/₄ teaspoon fine sea salt

Pinch white pepper, preferably freshly ground

9 ounces unblemished white mushroom caps, brushed clean with a soft brush and thinly sliced

2 tablespoons finely snipped chives, for garnish

To prepare the vinaigrette, in a mini food processor, combine the mustard, vinegar, lemon juice, pistachio oil, olive oil, tarragon leaves, salt, and pepper. Process until creamy. If desired, refrigerate for up to 6 hours before serving (the flavor will improve after an hour or two, as the flavors "marry").

To serve, chill 6 plates. Unwrap the salmon and scrape off the curing paste, then rinse briefly to get rid of any excess paste. Pat dry with paper towels and place flesh side up on a cutting board. Slice very thinly on the diagonal, preferably with a long, flexible, razor-sharp knife.

Divide the mushrooms among the plates, spreading them in an even, flat layer. Jumble 4 to 6 slices of salmon on top, twisting and curling them into a pretty, abstract mound. Drizzle each serving with about a tablespoon of the vinaigrette, scatter with a few chives, and serve.

For 6 servings: 299 calories, 4 grams net carbs (6 grams less 2 grams fiber), 19 grams fat (4 grams saturated)

For 8 servings: 224 calories, 4 grams net carbs (5 grams less 1 gram fiber), 14 grams fat (3 grams saturated)

Haricots Frites *with* Tarragon Sauce

SERVES 4 * A little more involved than my usual fare, this cocktail-hour snack was inspired by a luminous dinner at The Inn at Little Washington in Virginia. The beans were green and crisp yet yielding, with an ethereal tempuralike coating that I immediately vowed to re-create. This dish is to French fries what caviar is to canned sardines—save it for a night when you are out to impress.

TARRAGON DIPPING SAUCE

$1/4$ cup seasoned rice vinegar

$1/4$ cup chicken broth

2 teaspoons tamari or low-sodium soy sauce

1 teaspoon Thai or Vietnamese fish sauce (optional)

$1/2$ teaspoon minced fresh tarragon

8 ounces fine French green beans, ends trimmed

$1/4$ cup rice flour

1 teaspoon all-purpose flour

$1/3$ cup cold water

Vegetable oil, for deep frying

1 large egg white

$1/4$ teaspoon fine sea salt, plus more to taste

$1/8$ teaspoon fresh lemon juice, or $1/16$ teaspoon cream of tartar

To prepare the dipping sauce, in a bowl or serving cup, stir together the rice vinegar, chicken broth, tamari, fish sauce, and tarragon.

Prepare an ice bath. In a pot of rapidly boiling, salted water, blanch the beans for 3 minutes, drain, and plunge into the ice water. Let stand for 2 minutes, then drain again and spread on a kitchen towel to dry. (The beans can be covered and refrigerated for up to 2 hours before frying.)

Place the rice flour and all-purpose flour in a bowl and whisk with a fork while you dribble in a little cold water; whisk to a paste before you add more water, and keep whisking to banish any lumps until all the water has been added. Let stand for at least 15 minutes, and up to 45 minutes. Whisk again to distribute the flour evenly just before using.

Place a large, heavy saucepan or a wok filled no more than one-third full with vegetable oil over high heat, and heat the oil to between 350°F and 375°F.

Just before you plan to fry the beans, in a large bowl, beat the egg white with $1/4$ teaspoon salt to stiff peaks, adding the lemon juice after a minute or two. With a rubber spatula, fold the egg whites into the flour-water mixture until smooth and thick. Dip one third of the beans about halfway into the batter and slide gently into the hot oil. Fry for about 2 minutes, until the batter is crisp, slightly puffed, and pale golden, not dark brown. With a skimmer, transfer the finished frites to a paper towel–lined plate, salt lightly, and keep warm in a low oven while you fry the remaining beans in the same way (be sure to bring the oil back up to temperature between batches, or the frites will be soggy). Place all the frites on a platter with the dipping sauce in the center and serve warm.

57 calories, 8 grams net carbs (11 grams less 3 grams fiber), 0 grams fat (0 grams saturated)

Soups

The main benefit of soups to the low-carb gourmet —other than great flavor, comfort, and superb presentation —is that they are very filling.

ETHEREAL OR EARTHY, rich or feather-light, briny or meaty, there is a soup for all seasons, for all tastes, and for all levels of kitchen ambition. The main benefit of soups to the low-carb gourmet—other than great flavor, comfort, and superb presentation—is that they are very filling. A cup or two of soup and your cup may, um, runneth over. Teach yourself to see soup not just as a predinner option but also as an instead-of-dinner or lunch choice. Soups like Three-Onion Soup with Parmesan Frico (page 35) and Pumpkin Purée with a Pancetta Crisp (page 36) are natural choices for a winter soup-and-salad lunch or dinner, while Greek Zucchini Soup (page 34) and Garlic and Green Pea Vichyssoise (page 38) admirably fill the same roles in summertime.

On a rainy weekend, make your own chicken, veal, or beef stock, using a recipe from one of the good chef's books, and freeze it 1-pint portions for future soups. It will make the most arresting difference in the quality of your soups. (Making stock is a very Zen pursuit, even better than cleaning 3 pounds of shrimp or topping-and-tailing 5 pounds of green beans.)

It was my friend Jean-François Méteigner, chef/owner of La Cachette restaurant in Los Angeles who taught me that soups were a fantastic tool in the pursuit of weight-loss. His restaurant is renowned for its tasty, modern approach to classic French cooking, in which almost no butter and very little cream are used. Yet the food never seems obviously dietetic, and continues to appeal year after year (he was the chef at, arguably, Los Angeles' best restaurant L'Orangerie for many years, so his chops—as it were—are substantial).

"Soups fill you up without too many calories," he would say in his thick and charming French accent as we sat in his pretty restaurant working on his cookbook (*Cuisine Naturelle,* from Putnam Books). Jean-Francois had very specific ideas about soup, and through him I discovered that without cream, an credibly fluffy and creamy consistency can be achieved with that muscular powerhouse of blenders, the Vita-Mix.

He also spoke at what seemed to be great length about the safety concerns of blending hot soups.

"Let the soup cool for ten minutes, then hold the top of the blender very, very firmly with a folded towel before you begin blending," he would shout, each time we worked on a soup recipe.

"What's the deal J.F., aren't we going a little overboard?" I asked.

Well, apparently several years earlier he had been teaching a cooking class when a hot soup exploded from the blender, showering several people in the front row with molten liquid. No one was amused, and ever since, he has made it his mission in life to prevent it from happening again.

Deconstructed Lobster Gazpacho

SERVES 4 * This interactive, sparkling variation of the gazpacho I came to love during the long, hot summers on the Costa del Sol always elicits oohs and ahs of surprise and appreciation. The riotous flavors, brilliant colors, and briny lobster will make you forget that the soup is missing that traditional Andalusian ingredient: bread. The more perfectly you dice your ingredients for this soup ($1/8$-inch pieces are preferred), the more beautiful it will be.

4 large cloves garlic, minced or pressed

1 teaspoon fine sea salt

$1/4$ teaspoon cayenne pepper

3 tablespoons tomato paste

$2 1/4$ teaspoons white wine vinegar

$1/4$ cup best-quality extra virgin olive oil, preferably from Spain

$2 1/4$ teaspoons fresh lemon juice

$2 1/4$ cups tomato juice

1 sprig fresh thyme

8 ounces cooked lobster, cut into $1/4$-inch dice

1 cup finely diced peeled tomatoes (see Note)

1 cup finely diced green bell pepper (remove all seeds and white ribs before dicing)

1 cup finely diced peeled European cucumber

$3/4$ cup finely diced red onion

In a large glass measuring cup, whisk together the garlic, salt, cayenne, tomato paste, vinegar, olive oil, lemon juice, and tomato juice. Add the thyme, cover with plastic wrap, and refrigerate overnight, for the flavors to marry.

One hour before serving, prepare the remaining ingredients and place everything except the lobster in 4 separate small and attractive serving bowls. Chill thoroughly. Also chill 4 wide, shallow soup bowls, 4 small serving spoons, and 4 soup spoons.

Just before serving, remove the thyme sprig and whisk the tomato juice mixture well. Place in an attractive glass or ceramic pitcher. Divide the diced lobster evenly among the chilled bowls, mounding it in the center. Place the bowls of diced vegetables on the table, with a cold spoon for each one. Pass the garnishes and the pitcher of juice, so guests can pour the juice over the lobster, then select and create their own vegetable garnish for the gazpacho.

NOTE: If you can get really ripe, red tomatoes, peel, seed, and dice them for this dish. Otherwise, use canned San Marzano or other Italian plum tomatoes; drain and seed them before chopping. To peel fresh tomatoes, cut a shallow cross on the bottom of each tomato and submerge in boiling water for about 10 seconds to loosen the skin. Drain immediately and stop the cooking by running under cold water. The skins will slip off easily.

245 calories, 15 grams net carbs (18 grams less 3 grams fiber), 15 grams fat (2 grams saturated)

Radicchio Purée *with* Lemon-Chive Aïoli

SERVES 4 TO 6 ∗ If the only way you've eaten radicchio is raw, you owe it to yourself to explore the bittersweet possibilities of cooked radicchio (grilling is a surprising natural for this sturdy non-green, non-lettuce salad leaf). Occupying the space that would normally be taken by potatoes, cauliflower acts as a savory, thick base in this earthy fall soup. If you can spare a few extra carbohydrates, you can make the soup with 4 ounces of peeled, cored, and chopped apple instead. Substituting apple for cauliflower will increase the total carb count by 14 grams.

2 teaspoons olive oil

1 ounce pancetta or prosciutto, coarsely chopped

Half a small white or yellow onion, finely chopped

1 small carrot, finely chopped

2 bay leaves

1 medium head radicchio, about 12 ounces, quartered, cored, and cut into ¹/₂-inch slices (reserve 2 tablespoons of slivered radicchio for the garnish)

¹/₄ teaspoon fine sea salt, plus more to taste

¹/₄ teaspoon freshly ground black pepper, plus more to taste

2¹/₂ cups chicken broth or beef consommé, or half of either one and half water

4 ounces cauliflower florets (about 1¹/₄ cups), coarsely chopped

¹/₃ cup heavy whipping cream

LEMON-CHIVE AÏOLI

¹/₂ cup Aïoli-Mayo Base (page 150), or store-bought mayonnaise

1 teaspoon minced lemon zest

1¹/₂ tablespoons finely snipped chives

Place a large, heavy saucepan over low heat and add the olive oil. Add the pancetta and sauté gently, stirring, for 2 to 3 minutes, until most of the fat has rendered out. Add the onion, carrot, and bay leaves and cook gently for about 5 minutes, until the onion is softened. Add the radicchio, salt, and pepper and cook for about 4 minutes, until the radicchio has wilted.

Add the chicken broth, bring to a simmer, and add the cauliflower. Partially cover and cook gently for 20 minutes, until the cauliflower is very tender. Remove from the heat and let stand for 10 minutes, uncovered. Retrieve and discard the bay leaves and purée, preferably in a Vita-Mix blender, for about 30 seconds, until completely smooth. Wipe the pan with a paper towel, return the soup to the pan, and stir in the cream. Bring to a gentle simmer and taste for seasoning. Simmer for 3 minutes more, to thicken and reduce slightly.

To prepare the aïoli, in a bowl, whisk together the aïoli-mayo base, lemon zest, and chives until smooth (if using store-bought mayonnaise, thin to a consistency slightly thicker than heavy cream with a teaspoon or two of water). If desired, transfer to a squeeze bottle.

Ladle the soup into wide, shallow soup bowls and garnish with generous drizzles and swirls of the aïoli. Scatter with a few slivers of raw radicchio and serve at once.

For 4: 368 calories, 9 grams net carbs (10 grams less 1 gram fiber), 36 grams fat (9 grams saturated)

For 6: 245 calories, 6 grams net carbs (7 grams less 1 gram fiber), 24 grams fat (6 grams saturated)

Napa Cabbage *and* Mahogany Duck Consommé

SERVES 6 * After college, I spent a year in New York's Little Italy, mere blocks away from my other favorite place to shop for provisions, Chinatown. I soon came to see those lacquered, savory ducks hanging in the windows of the little shops as a convenient boon for a busy gourmet. In this soup, the sweet, succulent meat is submerged in a rich broth, while the mahogany skin scattered on top adds texture and flavor. If you don't live near a Chinatown, wash, dry, and roast a duck according to any good recipe, brushing the skin all over with an equal mixture of honey and soy sauce two or three times during the last 20 minutes. And if you don't mind an extra 6 grams of carbohydrates per head, divide 2 ounces (uncooked weight) of cooked rice stick or bean thread noodles among the 4 bowls after ladling in the broth.

6 cups chicken broth

8 ounces chicken parts, such as wing tips or backs

3 pods star anise

3 sprigs cilantro

3 sprigs flat-leaf parsley

2 tablespoons Thai or Vietnamese fish sauce, plus more to taste

1 tablespoon tamari or low-sodium soy sauce, plus more to taste

4 cups (loosely packed) finely julienned napa cabbage

Half a Chinatown duck, cut into small serving pieces (ask the duck salesman to do this for you; he has a razor-sharp cleaver)

¼ cup hoisin sauce, for serving

4 green onions, crisp green parts only, thinly sliced

2 tablespoons finely chopped cilantro, for serving

In a large saucepan, combine the broth, chicken parts, star anise, cilantro, parsley, fish sauce, and tamari. Bring to a gentle simmer, partially cover the pan, and let cook very gently for 45 minutes. Strain into a clean pan through a fine-meshed sieve. (The consommé can be cooled to room temperature and refrigerated for up to 2 days before serving.)

Just minutes before serving, bring the consommé to a gentle simmer and stir in the cabbage. Simmer for 1 minute, then taste for seasoning and adjust with fish sauce and tamari if necessary. Divide the duck pieces among 6 deep bowls and ladle the hot consommé and cabbage over the top. Drizzle the hoisin sauce back and forth across the top of the soup, scatter with the green onions and cilantro, and serve.

161 calories, 12 grams net carbs (13 grams less 1 gram fiber), 10 grams fat (3 grams saturated)

Greek Zucchini Soup

SERVES 4 * This Greek soup is a gift that, unlike the ubiquitous, piney-scented retsina, travels very well. It is far more than the sum of its parts and must be tried to be understood. At first, add only half the lemon juice specified, then taste before adding more juice, a teaspoonful at a time, until you find the perfect balance. Remember, though, that this soup's charm is in its bracing pucker.

3^1/$_2$ cups chicken broth, preferably homemade

^{1}/$_4$ cup water

2 tablespoons dry white wine

8 ounces small zucchini (about 2), washed, trimmed, and sliced ^{1}/$_4$ inch thick

2 large eggs, at room temperature

^{2}/$_3$ cup fresh lemon juice

^{1}/$_2$ teaspoon fine sea salt

Pinch of white pepper, preferably freshly ground

In a medium saucepan, combine the chicken broth, water, wine, and zucchini. Over medium-high heat, bring to a boil and adjust the heat so the liquid simmers. Cook for about 5 minutes, until the zucchini is tender but still bright green. Holding the top on very firmly with a folded towel to prevent an explosion, purée the mixture in a blender until completely smooth. In a large bowl, whisk together the eggs and lemon juice, then whisk in the puréed broth mixture until smooth. Return the mixture to the pan and place over low heat. Whisking all the time, cook until the soup thickens slightly, to a thin coating consistency. Do not allow it to boil. (To be safe, use a thermometer and be sure the mixture does not exceed 180°F.) Stir in the salt and pepper.

As soon as the soup is ready, remove from the heat and serve at once, to preserve the lovely bright green of the zucchini.

96 calories, 5 grams net carbs (6 grams less 1 gram fiber), 6 grams fat (2 grams saturated)

Three-Onion Soup *with* Parmesan Frico

SERVES 4 ✳ At once healthy yet very substantial, this soup is a fantastic addition to the low-carb repertoire—it's like a traditional French onion soup that has been to the Sorbonne. The frico can be a snack or a garnish, or it can even be crumbled to replace bread crumbs. When you crave the crunch that is hard to find when we stop eating fried starches, frico roars to the rescue. Do not, however, attempt to make them without a nonstick pan or with commercially grated domestic Parmesan.

3 tablespoons unsalted butter

2 large white onions (about 1³/₄ pounds), halved lengthwise and very thinly sliced

1 red onion (about ¹/₂ pound), thinly sliced

7 tablespoons amontillado (medium-dry) sherry

3 cups homemade chicken broth or canned low-sodium chicken broth

3 cups canned beef consommé

¹/₂ teaspoon fine sea salt

Freshly ground black pepper

1 green onion, light and dark green parts only, thinly sliced on the diagonal

FRICO
¹/₂ cup fresh coarsely grated Parmigiano-Reggiano or grana padano cheese, firmly packed (2 to 3 ounces)

Place a large saucepan over medium heat and add the butter. When it is melted, add the onions and cook, stirring frequently, until softened and nicely browned, about 15 minutes. Add 2 tablespoons of the sherry and reduce the heat to medium-low. Cook, stirring occasionally, until evaporated, and add another 2 tablespoons of sherry. Cook until evaporated and repeat once more. Continue cooking and stirring the onions until they are deep brown, about 10 minutes more.

Add the chicken broth and the consommé and bring to a boil, then adjust the heat so the liquid simmers gently. Stir in the salt and a few grinds of pepper. Simmer, partially covered, for 1 hour, until the onions are very tender. Stir in the last tablespoon of sherry and remove from the heat. Cover the pan while you make the frico.

Preheat the oven to 350°F (do not use the convection feature, if you have it). Lightly oil a nonstick baking sheet. Using 2 tablespoons of the coarsely grated cheese, make a circle on the baking sheet about 4 inches in diameter. Pat and spread the cheese gently into a thin, even layer—there will be a few tiny gaps, but they'll fill in when the cheese melts. Make 3 more circles with the remaining cheese. Bake the frico for 4 to 5 minutes, until bubbling, lacy, and still pale. Do not overcook, or the frico will be bitter and brittle. Remove from the oven and let stand for 1 minute, then loosen the edges with a nonstick spatula and transfer the frico gently to a paper towel to harden and remove the excess oil. (The frico will keep in an airtight container for 5 days.) Ladle the soup, with plenty of onions, into wide, shallow soup bowls, and at the last minute, gently float a frico in the center of each one.

285 calories, 14 grams net carbs (16 grams less 2 grams fiber), 16 grams fat (9 grams saturated)

Pumpkin Purée *with a* Pancetta Crisp

SERVES 4 * This colorful soup—made in the French style with plenty of wine—is perfect for the chill months of fall when your fast-slimming body cries out for comforting, substantial foods. I learned to make pancetta crisps while writing the Patina cookbook with Joachim Splichal, a chef who has a way of turning ingredients upside down, presenting them in unexpectedly pleasing new ways.

4 slices pancetta ¹/₈-inch thick (this is thicker than pancetta is normally cut)

3 tablespoons unsalted butter

1 large onion, finely chopped

1 leek, white part only, well washed and finely chopped

Large sprig or branch of fresh thyme

1¹/₂ pounds peeled, seeded, and coarsely chopped pumpkin or kabocha squash (from about 2¹/₄ pounds pumpkin)

2 cups dry white wine

¹/₂ teaspoon fine sea salt

Generous pinch of white pepper, preferably freshly ground

Preheat the oven to 300°F. Place the pancetta on a parchment-lined baking sheet and top with another sheet of parchment and a baking sheet that is the same size or that will sit flat on top of the paper. Bake for 45 to 50 minutes, until golden brown and crisp. Transfer to paper towels and set aside until serving time. (Begin making the soup while the crisps are cooking, if desired.)

In a large saucepan, melt the butter over medium-low heat. Add the onion, leek, and thyme and cook gently without browning for about 5 minutes, until translucent. Add the pumpkin, partially cover the pan, and cook for 10 minutes. Check occasionally and add a few tablespoons of water if the pumpkin begins to brown. Add the wine, adjust the heat so the liquid simmers briskly, and cook until reduced by half, about 20 minutes. Add 2 cups of water, partially cover the pan, and simmer for about 35 minutes, until the pumpkin is very tender. Remove from the heat and let cool, uncovered, for 5 minutes. Remove the thyme branch and purée the pumpkin mixture in a blender (preferably a Vita-Mix, for the fluffiest result). Purée in batches if necessary, until completely smooth. Work the purée through a medium sieve to remove any fibers and make the soup silky smooth. Return to the pan and stir in the salt and pepper. Warm through gently, then divide among 4 shallow soup bowls. Float a pancetta crisp in the center of each, and serve.

238 calories, 12 grams net carbs (15 grams less 3 grams fiber), 10 grams fat (6 grams saturated)

Garlic and Green Pea Vichyssoise

SERVES 4 * The previous two soups are all about fall and winter, but this lovely, filling soup trumpets summer with pale and elegant notes. I created it for my friend Siri's magazine *Garden Compass* when she asked for a soup that took advantage of the summer garden's bounty. Serve it in delicate soup bowls, perhaps with pale green napkins, fine stemware, and a light and grassy trebbiano or an easier-to-find pinot grigio from Orvieto. The soup can be served warm if desired; do not simmer the soup for more than a minute after adding the pea purée, or the bright flecks of green will turn dull.

2 heads fresh green garlic, or 6 cloves elephant garlic

1 tablespoon extra virgin olive oil

4 cups water

1^1/$_2$ cups whole milk

2 tablespoons unsalted butter

2 large leeks, white and tender green parts only, well washed and thinly sliced

8 ounces cauliflower florets (about 2^1/$_2$ cups), coarsely chopped

^{1}/$_2$ cup heavy whipping cream

1 teaspoon fine sea salt

^{1}/$_2$ teaspoon white pepper, preferably freshly ground

^{1}/$_2$ cup frozen petits pois, completely thawed (or use fresh garden peas, blanched just until tender, 1 to 2 minutes)

2 ounces salmon roe (optional)

Peel and coarsely chop the garlic. In a medium saucepan, warm the oil over very low heat (use a flame tamer if your burner is difficult to control at extremely low heat). Add the garlic and cook, stirring often, for about 20 minutes, or until the garlic is soft and translucent. Do not let it brown.

Add the water and milk and bring to a boil over high heat. Lower the heat and simmer very gently, partially covered, for 40 minutes. The garlic will be very tender.

While the garlic broth is simmering, melt the butter in a large saucepan over medium-low heat. Add the leeks and cauliflower and cook, partially covered, stirring occasionally, for about 10 minutes, until the vegetables are tender but not at all browned. Add the garlic broth and the cream, salt, and pepper. Bring the soup to a simmer and cook, partially covered, for 25 minutes more. Let cool slightly, and purée in a blender (preferably a Vita-Mix, for the fluffiest result) until smooth. Pass through a strainer into a bowl, pushing and scraping to remove the leek fibers. Cool to room temperature, cover, and chill for at least 4 hours and up to overnight.

In a food processor, purée the peas until very smooth, scraping down the sides as necessary. Stir the pea purée into the cold soup. Serve the soup in chilled bowls, garnished with a spoonful of salmon roe, if desired.

309 calories, 17 grams net carbs (20 grams less 3 grams fiber), 24 grams fat (13 grams saturated)

Oyster Bisque

SERVES 4 * Jeremiah Tower is one of my heroes. Since his first book, when I was an enthusiastic ama-
teur in England, his food has never ceased to inspire me and bring me back into the kitchen. His
delightful recent writing is all about honest, warts-and-all hedonism, and it happily reminds me of
me. I'm indebted to him for the idea for this light but luxurious soup—one of the easiest and most
elegant of all time. Use the Pacific oysters sold in jars for this dish if you are afraid—or don't know
how—to shuck oysters, but use only seven, since they are so very much larger.

15 freshly shucked medium-sized
oysters, with their liquor

2 tablespoons unsalted butter

1¹/₂ cups half-and-half

¹/₂ cup heavy whipping cream

¹/₈ teaspoon fine sea salt, plus more
to taste

Pinch of white pepper, preferably
freshly ground, plus more to taste

¹/₄ cup domestic or imported caviar,
for garnish (optional)

4 teaspoons finely snipped chives

Warm 4 shallow bowls in a low oven (the soup looks particularly
nice in glass bowls).

In a heavy saucepan, combine the oysters, butter, half-and-
half, cream, salt, and white pepper. Place the pan over high heat
and bring just to the bubbling point, then remove from the heat.
(Watch carefully: it can boil up and over within seconds, which
will not only toughen the oysters but also make a mess.)

Let the soup stand for 1 minute, then pour into a blender
(preferably a Vita Mix, for the fluffiest result). Holding the top of
the blender on securely with a folded towel, purée for about 30
seconds, then taste for seasoning and divide among the warm
bowls. Scatter the top with caviar and chives over the top and
serve at once.

*321 calories, 10 grams net carbs (10 grams less 0 grams fiber),
25 grams fat (14 grams saturated)*

When you leave behind the outmoded notion that oil is a bad thing, salad options become luscious, delicious, and almost as varied as the offerings at a good farmers' market.

I COULD LIVE ON SALAD, and I sometimes dine alone in front of a black-and-white movie on a huge Caesar (substituting frico, page 35, for the croutons, of course). When you leave behind the outmoded notion that oil is a bad thing, salad options become luscious, delicious, and almost as varied as the offerings at a good farmers' market. Please, add protein to your salads, particularly if you are not serving it elsewhere in the menu. Then you have the free food (the greens) that also contain our desperately needed fiber, a melodious dressing, and seafood, meat, or poultry to jazz it up—and, incidentally, to fill you up. See your leftover protein as a composed salad opportunity: Didn't finish all your steak the night before? Slice it and add it to the side of the plate. Just be sure to return the protein to room temperature before adding it to your salad.

Some of the salads in this chapter can stand alone as a main course (Grilled Calamari, Chorizo, and Artichoke Salad with Paprika-Lemon Vinaigrette, page 50, or Escarole with Duck Sausage, Blue Cheese, and Warm Walnut Oil Vinaigrette, page 43). Some are meant to accompany a rich and complex main course (Butter Lettuce and Fresh Tarragon with Dijon Vinaigrette, page 46, or Wilted Cabbage Salad with Warm Red Onion and Sherry Vinaigrette, page 49). Others are designed to precede a simple main course, like the life-changing Burrata and Seared Fig Salad with Prosciutto (page 44). Most of the salads are quick to assemble, with the worthwhile exceptions of the Heirloom Tomatoes with Homemade Ricotta and Mâche (page 48) and the Bacon, Portobello Mushroom, and Deep-Fried Egg Frisée Salad (page 53). It's an eclectic and pleasing collection, with something for every season, taste, and energy level.

Escarole *with* Duck Sausage, Blue Cheese, *and* Warm Walnut Oil Vinaigrette

SERVES 4 * This fast, easy salad is one hundred percent winter food, and it embodies all the things I like about the low-carb way of life. Rustic and satisfying without being heavy, it puts the lie to that old wives' tale about starchy, heavy food being the best choice for a cold season. It combines slightly bitter greens, a nutty dressing, fragrant and rich yet lean duck sausage, and the surprising earthy tang of blue cheese lurking under the leaves. If you use precooked duck sausage—now widely available—you can skip the poaching step.

5 cups water, chicken broth, white wine, or any combination

8 ounces fresh duck sausage (about 2 links), in the casings

7 to 8 ounces pale inner leaves from 1 head of escarole (about 8 cups, very loosely packed), washed and dried

1 tablespoon finely diced red onion (optional)

6 tablespoons walnut oil

2 tablespoons white wine vinegar

1 clove garlic, minced or pressed

1/2 teaspoon granular Splenda

1/4 teaspoon fine sea salt

Freshly ground black pepper

3 ounces best-quality blue cheese, crumbled

Bring the water to a slow simmer in a large saucepan (there should be enough liquid to cover the sausages by 1/2 inch). Add the sausages and poach for 4 minutes, then drain on paper towels. When cool enough to handle, slice them about 1/2 inch thick.

Preheat a ridged cast-iron grill pan over high heat. When the surface is very hot, sear the sausage slices for 21/2 minutes, turning them over halfway through, until nicely marked from the ridges of the pan. Cool briefly, then cut in half crosswise.

Tear the escarole into large, bite-sized pieces and arrange on a platter. Scatter the sausage and red onion over the top.

In a small saucepan, combine the walnut oil, vinegar, garlic, Splenda, salt, and several grinds of pepper. Bring to a simmer, whisking with a fork, and immediately drizzle over the salad. Toss the salad gently but thoroughly, scatter the blue cheese over the top, and serve with tongs, distributing the ingredients evenly.

402 calories, 2 grams net carbs (3 grams less 1 gram fiber), 33 grams fat (9 grams saturated)

Burrata *and* Seared Fig Salad *with* Prosciutto

SERVES 4 * This salad incorporates two passionate—but difficult—loves of mine: burrata cheese and fresh figs. Burrata is a sort of cross between fresh mozzarella and butter, and has only recently become available in large urban centers. It is highly perishable, so it doesn't ship well. Fresh mozzarella or, better yet—buffalo mozzarella—can happily be substituted. Figs are that rare fruit that is available only in its own true local season. Between the two, it's pretty certain you won't be making this salad in any season other than high summer, possibly early fall. Don't waste good, aged balsamic on this recipe; reducing it by half, actually makes indifferent supermarket balsamic taste like the 25-year-old stuff.

DRESSING

Scant $^1/_2$ teaspoon fine sea salt

Freshly ground black pepper

$1^1/_2$ tablespoons raspberry vinegar

$1^1/_2$ teaspoons cassis-flavored or cranberry-flavored Dijon mustard

$^1/_4$ cup extra virgin olive oil

2 tablespoons white truffle oil

1 teaspoon canola oil

4 ripe figs, stemmed and halved lengthwise (see Note)

4 cups (about 4 ounces) mâche (corn salad) or mild baby salad greens

4 large, paper-thin slices prosciutto

4 ounces very fresh burrata or fresh cow or buffalo mozzarella

4 teaspoons warm, slightly reduced balsamic vinegar (see Note)

Chill 4 salad plates and salad forks.

To prepare the dressing, in a large mixing bowl, combine the salt and several turns of the peppermill, the raspberry vinegar, mustard, olive oil, and truffle oil. With a small whisk, whisk briskly until creamy and emulsified. Set aside.

Place a heavy sauté pan or a cast-iron skillet over medium heat and add the canola oil. When the pan is hot, add the figs, cut sides down, and sear for 1 to 2 minutes, until golden brown and crusty, but not blackened. Remove the pan from the heat and leave the figs sizzling while you add the mâche to the mixing bowl and toss gently but thoroughly until evenly coated.

Divide the mâche among the chilled plates and drape a slice of prosciutto over the top. With a large spoon, scoop up a chunk of burrata (about a tablespoon) or cut the buffalo mozzarella into 8 equal chunks, and place one spoonful or chunk on either side of the salad. Place 2 figs, cut sides up, on each plate, drizzle the slightly warm balsamic syrup over the figs only, and serve at once.

NOTE: To reduce balsamic vinegar to a syrupy consistency, perfect for drizzling, gently simmer $^1/_2$ cup vinegar in a small saucepan until thickened. When cool, the syrup will be almost solid; warm it gently to achieve a flowing consistency. The syrup will keep almost indefinitely at room temperature; leave it in a small saucepan—like a butter warmer—until needed.

If fresh figs are unavailable, substitute dried figs (and note that this will increase the carb count by $2^1/2$ g per serving.

325 calories, 11 grams net carbs (13 grams less 2 grams fiber), 26 grams fat (6 grams saturated)

Butter Lettuce and Fresh Tarragon with Dijon Vinaigrette

SERVES 4 ∗ This recipe is so simple I feel a little embarrassed to include it. To achieve success with this classic, sophisticated salad choice, however, you must carefully follow the rules. Although it's been said countless times before, this truism bears repeating: When there are only a few ingredients in a dish, their quality is of supreme importance. Really good vinegar, the expensive olive oil you save for special occasions, the palest leaves of lettuce, and crisp, bright green tarragon leaves make this a salad that can pair with the most elegant protein dishes in your repertoire: perhaps a judiciously seasoned Dover sole, gently sautéed in French butter. On no account should this versatile dressing be made with domestic Dijon; the flavor is too weak. Search out Maille, Fauchon, or another imported French mustard.

VINAIGRETTE

2 tablespoons white wine vinegar

2 teaspoons imported Dijon mustard

$1/2$ teaspoon fine sea salt

Freshly ground black pepper

7 tablespoons extra virgin olive oil

3 crisp, unblemished heads butter lettuce, pale inner leaves only, washed and gently dried

2 teaspoons finely chopped fresh tarragon leaves

To prepare the vinaigrette, in a shallow salad bowl, combine the vinegar, mustard, salt, a few turns of the peppermill, and the olive oil. With a wire whisk, whisk constantly until a thickened and smooth emulsion forms. Set aside for up to 1 hour before serving, and whisk again just before adding the lettuce to reemulsify.

Just before serving, place the lettuce leaves in the salad bowl over the dressing (tear only the larger leaves; keep the smaller, cupped leaves intact). Toss gently but thoroughly to coat all the leaves evenly, inside and out, with the dressing. Scatter with the tarragon and serve at once.

220 calories, 1 gram net carbs (2 grams less 1 gram fiber), 23 grams fat (3 grams saturated)

Celery Hearts *and* White Anchovies *in* Green Olive Oil

SERVES 4 ∗ White anchovies bear as much resemblance to canned anchovies as, say, Lionel Poilâne's sourdough does to Wonder Bread. In Spain, one picked at them from little saucers placed near the sherry glasses. These dishes are called tapas because a saucer was often placed on top of a glass to keep out the flies, and someone had the bright idea of putting a nibble of salty, thirst-encouraging food on them. White anchovies, also called *boquerones en vinaigre,* are not particularly salty—they are plump, juicy, mild, and briny, the perfect foil for pale, yielding hearts of very fresh celery. The choice of olive oil is important here: splurge on a good one and this dish is likely to become an instant favorite, one that will please and surprise the most sophisticated gourmet. Once you become enamored of celery hearts there is, of course, the problem of what to do with the rest of the celery. Hmmmm . . . maybe you need a pet.

1 lemon, scrubbed to remove any wax

1 very fresh head best-quality celery

¹/₄ cup coarsely chopped flat-leaf parsley

2 to 4 tablespoons green, fruity, best-quality extra virgin olive oil, from Tuscany or Spain

Freshly ground black pepper

3 to 4 ounces mild Spanish white anchovies (available at specialty markets and websites); do not substitute standard anchovies

¹/₄ to ¹/₂ teaspoon Hawaiian orange salt (see Note)

Remove the lemon peel with a zester, making tiny curlicues of zest. Remove the outer stalks of celery, exposing the tender, very pale inner heart. Keep the celery stalks for another use, and with a large, sharp knife or a mandoline, sliver the celery hearts crosswise, including some but not all of the leafy tops. In a mixing bowl, combine the shaved celery hearts, lemon zest, parsley, 2 tablespoons of the olive oil, and a generous grinding of pepper. Toss thoroughly to combine, and arrange the salad down the center of a narrow oval platter. Halve the anchovies lengthwise and drape the slivers across the salad on the diagonal about ¹/₂ inch apart. If desired, drizzle back and forth with 2 more tablespoons of olive oil. Scatter with Hawaiian salt to taste and serve immediately, with a large, flat serving spoon or cake server.

NOTE: Orange salt is made by combining sea salt with Hawaii's mineral-rich clay.

146 calories, 2 grams net carbs (3 grams less 1 gram fiber), 12 grams fat (2 grams saturated)

Heirloom Tomatoes *with* Homemade Ricotta *and* Mâche

SERVES 6 ✳ Three of the chefs I've worked with influenced this elemental salad: Venice Beach's Joe Miller, who has been instrumental in bringing heirloom tomatoes into the mainstream; Evan Kleiman, an instinctual chef who introduced me to homemade ricotta (so delicate that the refrigerator's chill would compromise its flavor); and Jean-François Méteigner, who opened up a world of composed salads that—though they sound old-fashioned—are as up-to-the-minute as can be. Note that this homemade ricotta yields about 1 pound—more than you'll need—and makes a superb, slightly goaty kitchen snack (see page 11) all by itself.

RICOTTA

8 cups whole milk

1 cup goats' milk (optional)

1 cup heavy whipping cream (preferably not ultrapasteurized)

3¹/₂ tablespoons fresh lemon juice

Fine sea salt and freshly ground black pepper

2 tablespoons diced ripe yellow heirloom tomatoes (¹/₈-inch dice)

2 tablespoons diced ripe red heirloom tomatoes (¹/₈-inch dice)

2 tablespoons diced ripe purple heirloom tomatoes (¹/₈-inch dice) (if not available, increase the yellow tomatoes to 4 tablespoons)

4 ounces mâche (corn salad), roots removed, washed and spun dry

1 shallot, very finely chopped

2 tablespoons extra virgin olive oil

2 teaspoons walnut or sherry vinegar

To prepare the ricotta, about 2¹/₂ hours before serving, combine the milk, goats' milk, cream, and lemon juice in a large saucepan. Place over low heat and heat slowly, without stirring, to about 200°F (this will take 25 to 35 minutes). Line a small colander with a doubled thickness of slightly dampened cheesecloth (or use a large, fine-meshed sieve, without the cheesecloth). Place over a saucepan or 2-quart measure. As curds begin to form on the top of the liquid, stir the mixture gently and use a slotted spoon to transfer them to the colander. (If you prefer a large curd, don't stir the mixture too often; for this dish, a smaller curd is best.) When, eventually, more curds form above and below the surface (stir very gently every few minutes to see if they have formed yet), transfer them to the colander, or pour the entire mixture gently through the colander. Let the ricotta drain for 1 hour, until very thick.

Spoon about ¹/₃ cup of ricotta into the center of each plate and spread it into a thick, flat disk. Sprinkle each disk with a few grains of sea salt and a bit of pepper. Scatter the multicolored heirloom tomatoes around the edges of the plate. In a bowl, quickly but thoroughly toss the mâche with the shallot, olive oil, walnut vinegar, ¹/₄ teaspoon salt, and a pinch of pepper. Place a mound of the salad on top of the ricotta and serve at once.

190 calories, 3¹/₂ grams net carbs (4 grams less ¹/₂ gram fiber), 15 grams fat (7 grams saturated)

Wilted Cabbage Salad *with* Warm Red Onion *and* Sherry Vinaigrette

SERVES 4 * A cool-season salad, this surprising dish came into existence during an eleven-day stay in an electricity-less village in Baja California, where I celebrated the millennium New Year's Eve. The sun shone brightly, the tequila flowed generously, and we bought tuna within moments of its emergence from the impossibly blue sea. As for vegetables and lettuce, the town had none, except for cabbage in abundance. I'd arrived armed with my best collection of vinegars, some good mustard, and a jug of decent olive oil. Deciding that a cabbage and onion salad was better than braised cabbage and onions, I created this pretty salad.

Half a head of green cabbage, cored and thinly sliced (just under 1 pound)

1 medium leek, white and light green parts only, well washed, halved lengthwise, and cut into fine julienne

Half a large red onion, finely diced

$^1/_2$ teaspoon caraway seeds

$^1/_2$ cup extra virgin olive oil (do not use a top quality oil here)

Freshly ground black pepper

$1^1/_2$ tablespoons raspberry-flavored, cassis-flavored, or plain Dijon mustard

$^1/_2$ to $^3/_4$ teaspoon fine sea salt

2 to 3 tablespoons sherry vinegar

Half a red bell pepper, cored, seeded, deribbed, and finely diced

Place the sliced cabbage and leek in an attractive serving bowl. In a small saucepan, combine the onion, caraway seeds, olive oil, and a generous grinding of black pepper and place over medium heat. Bring up to a very gentle simmer and cook for 10 minutes, until the onion is tender. Stir in the mustard (don't worry if the mixture is lumpy) and pour the mixture over the cabbage. Immediately begin tossing the cabbage with tongs, tossing for a good 2 minutes, until the cabbage is wilted and glossy. Sprinkle with the salt and 2 tablespoons of the vinegar, and toss to distribute thoroughly. Taste for seasoning and add an additional $^1/_4$ teaspoon salt and/or 1 tablespoon vinegar if desired, tossing and tasting until the balance is perfect. Scatter with the red pepper and serve at once.

289 calories, 8 grams net carbs (11 grams less 3 grams fiber), 27 grams fat (4 grams saturated)

Grilled Calamari, Chorizo, and Artichoke Salad with Paprika-Lemon Vinaigrette

Serves 4 * Food writers bear a responsibility to make every recipe unique, appealing, and delicious, yet in every book there are a handful of dishes of which the author is inordinately proud. This dish is one of my favorites because it is earthy and rustic—my two favorite words—without being heavy, and contains several of the foods I love best. That they should turn out to go so well together was a delicious surprise.

The artichokes and calamari can also be seared on an outdoor grill, preferably a charcoal one, but they require such a short grilling time that it's hardly worth lighting up the coals, unless you're also cooking something else. (If you do use a grill, put a close-meshed grate on top of the regular grate to keep the calamari pieces from dropping through.)

Cook the calamari in batches, placing the pieces on the pan one at a time, and then immediately going back to turn over the first piece and so on, removing the first piece as soon as the last piece you added has been turned over.

VINAIGRETTE

4 cloves garlic

$^1/_3$ cup firmly packed cilantro leaves

$^1/_3$ cup firmly packed flat-leaf parsley leaves

$^1/_4$ cup fresh lemon juice

1 teaspoon fine sea salt

$^1/_8$ teaspoon cayenne pepper

$1^1/_2$ teaspoons paprika, preferably Spanish pimentón

$^3/_4$ teaspoon ground cumin

$^1/_2$ cup extra virgin olive oil

1 lemon, halved

8 baby artichokes or 4 large artichokes, stems left intact, well rinsed

To prepare the vinaigrette, turn on the motor of a food processor and toss in the garlic cloves one at a time, processing until they are finely minced and settled down. Add the cilantro, parsley, lemon juice, salt, cayenne, paprika, and cumin. Pulse until nice and chunky. With the motor running, add the olive oil and process until smooth. Cover and refrigerate for at least 1 hour and up to 3 hours before serving.

Fill a large pot with cold water and squeeze in the lemon juice, then drop in the lemon halves. One at a time, bend the lower leaves of each artichoke back on themselves until they snap. Continue until the pale, tender inner leaves are exposed, then cut off the top two thirds of the pointy end, about $^1/_2$ inch above the base. Trim off the woody ends of the stems, and peel the stems from the base upward with a vegetable peeler. With a small, sharp knife, trim off the tough, dark fibers that were left when you snapped off the leaves, trimming around in a circle without removing too much of the flesh. If desired, trim with a vegetable peeler to make a smooth surface. As you finish each artichoke, drop it into the lemon water and, when all of the 'chokes are trimmed, add the kosher salt, cover the pan, and bring

continued

1 tablespoon kosher salt

3/4 pound cleaned calamari tubes and tentacles (thawed frozen calamari is fine)

Olive oil, for brushing

Fine sea salt and freshly ground black pepper

2 ounces cured chorizo sausage, sliced 1/4 inch thick (or thinly sliced and halved crosswise)

to a boil. Adjust the heat and simmer until tender, about 15 minutes for baby artichokes, 25 for large ones. Drain upside down on a layer of paper towels and, when cool enough to handle, cut in half lengthwise and scoop out the choke, if any (baby artichokes sometimes don't have much of one). Cut large artichokes into quarters, and set aside.

With scissors, cut up one side of each calamari tube, open out flat, and pat dry with paper towels. Cut in half lengthwise and then again crosswise on a diagonal, into approximately 1 to 1 1/2-inch pieces. Leave the tentacles intact but make sure all are well dried.

Preheat a well-oiled cast-iron ridged grill pan over medium-high heat. Brush all sides of the calamari and artichokes lightly with olive oil and season with salt and pepper. Grill the calamari squares for about 30 seconds on each side and transfer to a large platter, then grill the artichokes, cut sides down, for about 2 minutes on each cut surface (1 surface for baby artichokes, 2 for large) until charred but not blackened. Transfer the artichokes to a plate, and grill the calamari tentacles until firm. Add the tentacles and chorizo to the calamari and drizzle generously with the vinaigrette. Toss together into an attractive jumble and pile high in the center of the platter. Arrange the artichokes around the calamari salad, smaller ends radiating outward. Drizzle around the artichokes with a little more vinaigrette and serve within 10 to 15 minutes, either still slightly warm or at room temperature.

440 calories, 11 grams net carbs (16 grams less 5 grams fiber), 35 grams fat (6 grams saturated)

Bacon, Portobello Mushroom, and Deep-Fried Egg Frisée Salad

SERVES 4 * During a trip to New Orleans, I experienced deep-fried poached eggs on bruschetta with winter greens at the lovely Herbsaint restaurant. A revelation! An impossibility! After grilling talented Donald Link without mercy, I persuaded the enthusiastic young chef to part with the secret of keeping the egg yolks runny even after their encounter with the hot oil. The trouble is, he gave no real details (this is an annoying habit I've noticed in several of the chefs I've worked with). After a testing day that my kitchen would rather forget, here is the result, ready for its close-up. Although much of the preparation can be done in advance, this is not a simple dish. Success depends on timing and a very delicate hand with the eggs (poach an extra egg for safety, in case one self-destructs in the breading process). When done right, the lovely, runny yolk will be encased in a crunchy, warm exterior. The yolk mingles with the tart dressing, and the meaty portobellos help satisfy the heartiest appetite. It's substantial enough for a main course.

SIMPLE VINAIGRETTE

$1^1/_2$ tablespoons fresh lemon juice

$^1/_4$ teaspoon fine sea salt

Freshly ground black pepper

1 large clove garlic, minced or pressed

1 teaspoon Dijon mustard

6 tablespoons extra virgin olive oil

2 tablespoons distilled or cider vinegar

4 extra-large or jumbo eggs

4 ounces slab bacon, preferably applewood smoked, rind removed and cut into $^1/_4$ by $^1/_4$ by 1-inch lardons (or thick-cut smoked bacon, cut crosswise into $^1/_4$-inch strips)

4 medium portobello mushrooms, stemmed, brown gills scraped away, and peeled

To prepare the vinaigrette, in a large mixing bowl, combine the lemon juice, salt, a few grinds of pepper, garlic, mustard, and olive oil. Whisk together with a small balloon whisk until creamy and emulsified. Set the bowl aside. (If poaching the eggs ahead of time, do not make the vinaigrette until just before the salad will be finished.)

Prepare an ice bath for the eggs, to stop the cooking quickly. In a large sauté pan with high sides and a tight-fitting lid, bring a generous amount of water to a rolling boil and add the vinegar. Break 1 egg into each of 2 saucers. Turn off the heat and immediately tip the saucers to slide out the eggs gently, just above the surface of the water. Quickly break the remaining 2 eggs into the saucers and add them in the same way, leaving plenty of space between the 4 eggs so the whites do not mingle. Quickly cover the pan and leave it undisturbed for exactly $2^1/_2$ minutes. With a slotted spoon, gently transfer the eggs to the ice bath, transferring them in the order they were placed in the pan. (At this point, the bowl of eggs and ice water can be refrigerated for up to 2 hours.) In any event, keep the eggs very cold until just before they are fried.

continued

2 teaspoons unsalted butter or olive oil, if needed

Vegetable or canola oil, for deep frying

8 to 12 ounces pale inner leaves of frisée, washed and thoroughly dried (about 8 to 12 cups, loosely packed)

About 1½ cups toasted wheat germ, for dredging (not all the wheat germ will be used)

4 Parmesan frico (optional, page 35), for serving

Place the bacon strips (lardons) in a saucepan of cold water and bring to a boil. Simmer for 3 minutes, then drain and pat dry with paper towels.

Place a large skillet over medium-low heat and add the lardons. Sauté, stirring occasionally, until they are golden but not dark brown (if you are obsessive, turn them with tongs to brown all sides evenly). Transfer to paper towels with a slotted spoon, leaving the pan on the heat. Add the mushrooms to the pan, rounded side down, cover the pan, and reduce the heat to low. Cook gently until the mushrooms are glossy and tender, turning them once or twice, about 5 minutes (add up to 2 teaspoons butter or oil if the rendered fat from the lardons is not sufficient). Remove from the heat and leave covered. Warm 4 plates in a low oven.

Half-fill a wok or heavy sauté pan with oil and bring to 365°F to 370°F over high heat (or use an electric deep-fryer). When the oil has almost reached the correct temperature, retrieve the poached eggs from the ice bath with great gentleness and delicacy. Rest them on a doubled layer of paper towels.

Whisk the vinaigrette again to reemulsify it, then add the frisée and lardons to the bowl and toss to coat evenly.

Working over a shallow bowl with one egg at a time, ease an egg onto one hand and sprinkle both sides generously with wheat germ, letting the excess fall into the bowl and turning the egg gently from hand to hand to coat it evenly. Using a slotted spoon, lower the egg into the oil, release it, and fry for 20 to 25 seconds, until just pale golden. Retrieve it again with the slotted spoon and place on the cupped side of a mushroom cap. Quickly fry the other 3 eggs in the same way, place an egg-topped mushroom on each warm plate, and mound some salad on the side, including plenty of lardons. If using, balance a frico on top of each egg and serve at once.

431 calories, 9 grams net carbs (13 grams less 4 grams fiber), 35 grams fat (7 grams saturated)

chapter 4

Without starch on the plate, sides must shine very brightly, and they must also be satisfying.

WHEN I HEAR PEOPLE SAY they get tired of eating steak and cheese on a low-carb diet, I want to tear my hair out. What about all the fantastic vegetables? Yes, starchy vegetables like potatoes, corn, sweet potatoes, and even carrots should be avoided, but think of the wealth of flawless leaves, pods, spears, and squashes that are ready and waiting to be conjured into a collection of mouthwatering side dishes. There are so many to choose from, and some—like mushrooms and eggplant—are so versatile and filling that you should absolutely abandon protein one night a week to take advantage of the garden's bounty. This chapter is the longest in the book because vegetables, not meat and cheese, should become the staples of your new, low-carbohydrate lifestyle.

When I talk about vegetables, I don't mean a few steamed green beans. Without starch on the plate, sides must shine very brightly, and they must also be satisfying. Why not follow the English maxim—which used to irritate me no end when I lived there—of "meat and two veg" on every plate? With a pan-seared filet mignon, choose stylish sides like Zucchini Fettuccine with Sweet Butter (page 62) and Steamed and Seared Belgian Endive (page 69). With a rustic, herb-strewn roast chicken, opt for earthy sides like Long-Cooked Broccoli with Black Olives (page 60) and Swiss Chard and Roquefort Gratin (page 70).

Comforting, Creamy, White Cauliflower Purée

SERVES 4 TO 6 * This is my version of the French classic *pommes aligote*, and the cheese even gets nice and stringy like an *aligote* right after you add it. Of course, every book that offers low-carbohydrate recipes has a cauliflower purée, because everyone seems so sad to have lost mashed potatoes from their diet, but my version is the best. I actually prefer this dish to mashed potatoes, and anecdotal evidence shows I am not alone.

1 small cauliflower (1$^1/_2$ to 1$^3/_4$ pounds), thick stalks and leaves discarded, separated into walnut-sized florets with about 1 inch of the stem attached

$^1/_4$ cup heavy whipping cream

4 ounces Gruyère cheese, coarsely grated

$^1/_2$ teaspoon fine sea salt

$^1/_8$ to $^1/_4$ white pepper, preferably freshly ground

In the top of a steamer set over simmering water, steam the cauliflower for 20 to 25 minutes, until completely tender (test with a small, sharp knife). In a food processor, combine the steamed cauliflower and the cream and purée until completely smooth, scraping down the sides. Transfer to the top of a double boiler set over simmering water and stir in the cheese, salt, and pepper. Serve immediately or hold for up to 30 minutes over hot but not simmering water, stirring occasionally. Or refrigerate for up to 6 hours and warm gently in a double boiler.

For 4: 214 calories, 6 grams net carbs (10 grams less 4 grams fiber), 15 grams fat (9 grams saturated)

For 6: 142 calories, 5 grams net carbs (7 grams less 2 grams fiber), 10 grams fat (6 grams saturated)

Long-Cooked Broccoli *with* Black Olives

SERVES 4 * I've long loved—but sometimes been bored by—broccoli. I'd never realized its affinity for salty ingredients like olives, anchovies, and capers until I had the idea of combining it with a bruschetta topping I found in an Australian magazine. When bread departed from my diet, I didn't want to lose this rustic green and salty concoction, so I've found other ways to use it. To serve it as a finger food, mound and compact the mixture into the hollows of large, steamed button or cremini mushrooms.

$1^{1}/_{2}$ pounds firm, unblemished, bright green broccoli

$^{1}/_{4}$ cup extra virgin olive oil

2 tablespoons unsalted butter

4 cloves garlic, minced or pressed

4 to 5 anchovy fillets

6 ounces (1 cup) brine-cured black olives, such as niçoise, pitted and coarsely chopped

Freshly ground black pepper

$^{1}/_{2}$ teaspoon fresh lemon juice or white wine vinegar

Bring a large pot of generously salted water to a boil. Trim the woody ends of the broccoli and cut into florets. Peel off the coarse outer skins from the stalks (it is easier to do this with a sharp knife than with a peeler). Halve the thick stalks lengthwise and slice them crosswise $^{1}/_{2}$ inch thick. Add the broccoli to the boiling water and cook for 6 to 7 minutes, until bright green and crisp-tender. Drain in a colander and run under plenty of cold water until the steam stops rising. Shake the colander gently, turn the broccoli out onto a thick kitchen towel, and let dry for a few minutes, or up to 40 minutes if desired.

About 30 minutes before serving, chop the broccoli very coarsely. Place a large sauté pan over low heat and add the oil and butter. When the butter has melted, add the garlic and anchovy and mash to break up the anchovy and distribute both flavorings in the oil. Add all of the chopped broccoli and sizzle very gently for 20 minutes. Turn over with a spatula only once or twice during the cooking time, so you don't break up all the florets. Add the olives and season generously with black pepper. Cook, turning once or twice, for 15 to 20 minutes more, until softened, golden brown in places, and very aromatic. Sprinkle with the lemon juice and serve.

401 calories, 8 grams net carbs (14 grams less 6 grams fiber), 37 grams fat (11 grams saturated)

Leek *and* Garlic Flan *in* Chard Leaves

SERVES 4 * This flan is creamy and satisfying, with a sweet, mellow garlic flavor. Its dark green, crinkly wrapping looks brilliant alongside a chicken dish like Pan-Fried Chicken Breasts with Sage and Ham Butter (page 109) or Wine-Braised Chicken Thighs with Green Olives and Herbs (page 110).

4 large or 6 smaller leaves firm, glossy Swiss chard, ends trimmed

$1/2$ cup peeled garlic cloves (about 1 medium head)

$1/2$ cup thinly sliced leek, white part only (about 1 medium leek)

4 ounces peeled celery root or cauliflower (about $1^1/4$ cups), cut into 1-inch cubes

$1^1/4$ cups whole milk

2 large eggs

$3/4$ cup heavy whipping cream

$1/2$ teaspoon fine sea salt

Pinch of white pepper, preferably freshly ground

Dash of Tabasco sauce, or to taste

Slice the leaves from the chard stems and reserve the stems for another use (see Note). Place the leaves in a colander and pour a large kettle of boiling water over them. When cool enough to handle, spread the leaves out on paper towels and set aside.

In a medium saucepan, combine the garlic, leeks, celery root, and milk and bring to a boil. Reduce the heat so that the liquid is just simmering, cover, and cook until very soft, about 20 minutes. Drain, reserving $1/2$ cup of the milk. Purée the drained vegetables in a food processor for 2 to 3 minutes, or until very smooth. Add the reserved milk, eggs, cream, salt, pepper, and Tabasco. Process until smooth.

Preheat the oven to 325°F. Generously butter four $3/4$-cup ramekins and line them with the chard leaves, crisscrossing and overlapping a little here and there as necessary and leaving some of the leaves overhanging to form the top. Ease the chard firmly into the corners and sides with your fingertips. Set the ramekins in a small roasting pan and bring a kettle of water to a boil for the bain-marie. Pour the flan mixture into the ramekins, filling them to within $1/4$ inch of the rim, and fill the roasting pan with boiling water so that it reaches halfway up the sides of the ramekins. Fold the overhanging leaves over the top (do not press down) and transfer the pan to the oven. Bake until the center of each flan is firm, about 45 minutes. Remove the ramekins from the bain-marie and let rest for 5 minutes. To serve, unmold each flan by inverting it onto a wide spatula, and sliding it onto a warm plate.

NOTE: Slice the chard stems crosswise $1/4$ inch thick, then sauté over low heat in a mixture of butter and olive oil until tender, about 10 minutes. Stir in a teaspoon of your favorite tapenade and serve warm.

305 calories, 12 grams net carbs (14 grams less 2 grams fiber), 26 grams fat (15 grams saturated)

Zucchini Fettuccine *with* Sweet Butter

SERVES 4 * This title may sound delusional, but the result is slippery, rich, and satisfying—just like real fettuccine. You can skip the one-minute blanching process, if desired, but I think it gives the zucchini just exactly the right texture. This is a fantastic choice to accompany a simply sautéed filet mignon with a few garlic mushrooms on the side. With a menu like this, it's hard to imagine anyone complaining that a low-carb regimen is boring. Choose small, firm zucchini, which will have fewer seeds.

1^1/$_2$ pounds small zucchini (about 6), ends trimmed, halved lengthwise

1^1/$_4$ teaspoons fine sea salt

2 tablespoons heavy whipping cream

2 tablespoons unsalted butter

^{1}/$_4$ teaspoon fresh lemon juice

Freshly ground black pepper

Lay the zucchini halves cut sides down. With a very sharp knife, slice the halves lengthwise slightly less than ^{1}/$_8$ inch thick to make "fettuccine." In a colander, combine the zucchini with 1 teaspoon of the salt and toss together. Set aside to drain for 15 minutes while you bring a saucepan full of water to a boil and place a large bowl of ice and water near the stove for an ice bath.

Add the zucchini to the boiling water and blanch for 1 minute, then drain immediately and plunge into the ice bath to halt the cooking process. Drain again and pat the zucchini dry gently with a towel. (This can be done up to 2 hours ahead of time; wrap the zucchini in the towel and refrigerate until just before serving time.)

Warm a shallow serving bowl in a low oven, if desired, or you can serve directly onto dinner plates.

Place a large sauté pan over low heat and add the cream and butter. When the butter melts, add the zucchini and cook, stirring occasionally, until the sauce thickens and coats the zucchini, about 2 minutes. Stir in the lemon juice, remaining ^{1}/$_4$ teaspoon salt, and a few grinds of pepper. Serve immediately.

116 calories, 3 grams net carbs (5 grams less 2 grams fiber), 9 grams fat (5 grams saturated)

Spinach *and* Aged White Cheddar Soufflé

SERVES 4 * My mother's cheese soufflé is the first food I remember falling in love with. Julia Child was my soufflé influence for about ten years, and during the Wall Street days I made an awful lot of salmon soufflés from her recipe in *Mastering the Art of French Cooking*. Here, I wanted a soufflé that was tasty enough to serve as a side dish *or* a main course. The rustic tang of aged cheddar made the difference between bland, nursery-style food and more grown-up fare. About two years ago, I started serving all my beloved soufflés in a gratin dish instead of a soufflé dish because it's faster and there is less chance of the soufflé falling. Pssst: Soufflés are the perfect low-carbohydrate food!

6 ounces fresh baby spinach leaves, washed and dried

3 tablespoons unsalted butter

1 shallot, finely chopped

2 tablespoons soy flour

1 cup whole milk

$1/4$ teaspoon fine sea salt

Freshly ground black pepper

4 eggs, separated, plus 1 additional egg white

$1/4$ cup crème fraîche

3 ounces aged white cheddar cheese, coarsely grated

$1/2$ teaspoon fresh lemon juice, or $1/4$ teaspoon cream of tartar

Bring a large pot of lightly salted water to a boil, and add the spinach. Boil for 1 minute, then immediately drain in a colander and rinse under cold running water. Grab walnut-sized pieces of spinach and firmly squeeze out as much water as possible. Repeat with the remaining spinach and chop finely.

Preheat the oven to 400°F and butter an $8^{1}/_{2}$ by 2-inch deep round baking dish, or an 11 by 7-inch glass or ceramic baking dish. In a large saucepan, melt the butter over medium heat. Add the shallot and sauté for 2 minutes, then add the flour and stir into a paste. Cook, stirring, for 2 minutes (do not let it brown). Away from the heat, whisk in the milk. Whisk until smooth, then return to low heat and bring to a simmer. Cook, stirring or whisking occasionally, for about 10 minutes, until slightly thickened, then stir in the salt and pepper. Remove from the heat and immediately whisk in the egg yolks. Stir in the crème fraîche, chopped spinach, and cheddar and set aside.

In a large, perfectly clean bowl, using an electric mixer, beat the 5 egg whites and lemon juice to stiff peaks, then thoroughly stir one quarter of the egg whites into the spinach mixture, to lighten it. Gently but thoroughly fold the spinach mixture into the egg whites, and turn the mixture into the prepared dish, smoothing the top. Place on a baking sheet and place in the center of the oven. Turn the oven down to 350°F and bake for 22 to 25 minutes, until risen, golden brown, and no longer jiggly in the center. Serve immediately, using a large spoon.

250 calories, 6 grams net carbs (7 grams less 1 gram fiber), 20 grams fat (11 grams saturated)

Savoy Cabbage *with* Whole-Grain Mustard, Pearl Onions, *and* Applewood-Smoked Bacon

SERVES 4 * Pork and cabbage have some sort of spiritual affinity for each other that simply should not be messed with. But this is no sulfurous, mushy cabbage dish: the savoy cabbage—a completely different animal than the usual green cabbage—is slightly undercooked so that it retains its luminous green color and fresh flavor. Substitute shredded young Brussels sprouts for a real flavor surprise. Regular bacon can be substituted in a pinch, but applewood-smoked bacon is worth seeking out because the flavor outstrips the bland, cured variety by miles.

10 ounces small inner leaves of savoy cabbage, from 1 small head

2 tablespoons unsalted butter, at room temperature

20 pearl onions, peeled (or thawed frozen pearl onions)

1/8 teaspoon fine sea salt plus 1/4 teaspoon

White pepper, preferably freshly ground

2 tablespoons chicken broth (canned is fine)

3 ounces applewood-smoked bacon, cut crosswise into 1/2-inch-wide strips

1 tablespoon whole-grain mustard

Prepare an ice bath in a large bowl. In a large saucepan of lightly salted, boiling water, blanch the cabbage leaves for 1 minute, then quickly drain and plunge them into the ice bath to stop the cooking. Drain again and pat dry with a kitchen towel. Cut out any large ribs and slice crosswise into 3/4-inch julienne.

In a small saucepan, heat 1 tablespoon of the butter over medium-high heat and add the pearl onions, 1/8 teaspoon salt, and a pinch of pepper. Sauté for 5 to 6 minutes, stirring frequently, until golden. Add the broth, cover the pan, and simmer until the onions are tender, about 6 minutes (thawed frozen onions will take only about 2 minutes). Remove from the heat and set aside.

Place a large saucepan over medium-low heat, add the bacon, and cook gently to render out almost all of the fat, without browning the bacon. Spoon off and discard about a tablespoon of the fat. With a slotted spoon, add the onions, 1/4 teaspoon salt, a pinch more pepper, and the cabbage. Cook, stirring, until the mixture is very hot, 2 to 3 minutes. Remove from the heat and add the mustard and the remaining tablespoon of butter. Stir constantly until the mixture is creamy, only a minute or so. Taste for seasoning and serve.

133 calories, 8 grams net carbs (12 grams less 4 grams fiber), 9 grams fat (4 grams saturated)

Eggplant *and* Goat Cheese Lasagnas

SERVES 4 * Perfecting this dish was something of an ordeal—the vision didn't immediately pan out. Eggplant is meaty enough to make a filling and satisfying side dish (and it feels starchy even if it isn't). It's handy for when you are serving a light protein course like fish or poultry, or no protein at all.

2 large globe eggplants, preferably long and thin

$1/4$ cup coarse sea salt

Olive oil, for brushing

Freshly ground black pepper

Best-quality dried oregano, for sprinkling

3 ounces soft, mild goat cheese, such as Montrachet

$1/3$ cup freshly grated imported pecorino, grana padano, or Parmigiano-Reggiano

3 ounces slivered fontina cheese

8 leaves fresh basil, cut into julienne

1 roasted red bell pepper, peeled and cut into $1/4$-inch julienne (see page 82)

1 tablespoon coarsely chopped flat-leaf parsley

Trim off the stems of the eggplants and peel them, leaving four $1/2$-inch-wide, lengthwise strips of peel around each one. Slice them crosswise about $5/8$ inch thick (you should have 12 nice slices). Gently combine the eggplant slices with the salt in a colander, distributing the salt with your fingers. Let drain for 20 minutes, then rinse briefly and pat dry thoroughly with kitchen towels.

Preheat the oven to 350°F and line a baking sheet with parchment paper. Place the slices in a single layer on the parchment, and brush them lightly with olive oil. Season generously with pepper and oregano and bake for 5 minutes, until slightly softened. Remove from the oven, leaving it on if you plan to finish the dish immediately (the slices can stand at room temperature for up to 2 hours).

Cut the goat cheese into 4 equal pieces. On the same baking sheet, choose the 4 largest eggplant slices as the bases. Place a piece of goat cheese in the center of each and top with a pinch of pecorino. Top each with a medium-sized slice of eggplant, and top this slice with one fourth of the slivered fontina, one fourth of the basil, and another pinch of pecorino. Top each with another eggplant slice and press the top layer gently but firmly with a flat spatula to compact the stack a little. Sprinkle with the remaining pecorino and cover the pan with foil.

Bake the lasagnas for 20 to 25 minutes, until warmed through, with the cheese bubbling slightly around the edges. Remove the foil and cook for 5 to 10 minutes more, if necessary, until soft enough to cut with a fork (the peel will be a little tough, but it looks far more interesting than completely peeled eggplant). To serve, place a small jumble of red pepper julienne on top of each lasagna and scatter with a little parsley.

228 calories, 8 grams net carbs (13 grams less 5 grams fiber), 14 grams fat (9 grams saturated)

Grilled Asparagus *with* Tomato-Lime Hollandaise

SERVES 6 * Asparagus is a gracious choice for any occasion, especially with something equally elegant like a piece of super-fresh, simply grilled fish. In the wintertime when beautiful blood oranges are available and tomatoes are not (or shouldn't be, anyway), substitute blood orange juice for the lime juice and water, and omit the diced tomatoes. Use a ridged grill pan or simply blanch the asparagus in boiling water until almost tender.

1¼ pounds asparagus (the diameter at the base should be not much smaller than a dime)

TOMATO-LIME HOLLANDAISE

2 tablespoons fresh lime juice

1½ tablespoons water

2 large egg yolks

14 tablespoons (7 ounces) unsalted butter, cut into 14 equal pieces, at room temperature

½ teaspoon fine sea salt

1 plum tomato, peeled, seeded, and cut into ⅛-inch dice

2 teaspoons finely snipped chives (optional)

Tiny pinch of cayenne pepper

Snap off the woody ends of the asparagus about 1 to 1½ inches above the base. Peel the next 2 inches with a vegetable peeler, peeling up toward the flower ends. Bring a large skillet of lightly salted water to a boil and simmer the asparagus for 4 minutes, then remove with tongs and drain on paper towels.

To prepare the hollandaise, in a nonreactive double boiler over gently simmering water, combine the lime juice, water, and egg yolks. Whisk gently for 1 to 2 minutes, until the liquid is frothy and has just begun to thicken (it should be about the consistency of yogurt). Whisk in a piece of butter. When it is absorbed, continue whisking in the butter, a piece at a time, waiting until one piece has been absorbed before adding the next. Do not let the mixture get too hot—it should steam but not even begin to simmer. If it does get too hot, remove the pan from the heat for a minute or two while still whisking. Stir in the salt, diced tomatoes, chives, and cayenne. Cover the pan and set aside at the back of the stove while you grill the asparagus. (Do not leave it over even a very low burner, or the sauce will separate.)

Grill the asparagus perpendicular to the bars of the grill grate (or use a well-seasoned ridged grill pan), turning to char them evenly, for 4 to 8 minutes, until golden brown but not charred. Serve the asparagus immediately, with the hollandaise drizzled on top or on the side.

VARIATION: To serve this dish using simmered instead of grilled asparagus, cook the spears for 6 minutes instead of 4, and skip the grilling step.

284 calories, 4 grams net carbs (6 grams less 2 grams fiber), 29 grams fat (17 grams saturated)

Steamed *and* Seared Belgian Endive

SERVES 4 ✳ If you have never cooked a member of the endive family (radicchio, endive, escarole), start with this recipe. The user-friendly and inspiring Gotham Bar and Grill cookbook includes a recipe for braised individual leaves of endive, but it requires sugar. I came up with this lovely alternative, in which the slow, gentle sizzling crisps each and every layer of the endive's interior. The prosciutto is minimal—it doesn't make the dish heavy or rich, just adds that fantastic cured-pork flavor to what is a natural dish for fall and wintertime dinners.

2 large or 4 small unblemished Belgian endives, blunt ends trimmed, halved lengthwise

Fine sea salt and freshly ground black pepper

2 thin slices prosciutto, cut lengthwise into 3/8-inch strips

3 tablespoons unsalted butter

1 teaspoon finely chopped flat-leaf parsley (optional)

In a steamer basket set over gently simmering water, steam the endives cut side down for about 15 minutes, until almost translucent. Drain cut side down on a paper towel–lined plate until just before serving.

Season both sides of the endives generously with salt and pepper. Wrap a long strip of prosciutto around each endive half in a very loose corkscrew pattern.

In a large, nonstick skillet or sauté pan, melt the butter over low heat. Add the endives, cut sides down (do this in 2 pans if necessary to avoid overcrowding). Sizzle gently without disturbing until golden brown, 10 to 12 minutes, then turn over carefully and sear on the rounded side for about 4 minutes more. Scatter with a little parsley and serve within 5 minutes.

125 calories, 8 grams net carbs (9 grams less 1 gram fiber), 10 grams fat (6 grams saturated)

Swiss Chard and Roquefort Gratin

SERVES 4 * This is a nice alternative to potato gratin, and the presence of chives and crème fraîche takes away the heavy, cloying flavor that can accompany blue cheeses if we're not careful to balance the richness of this tasty—when taken in small doses—cheese.

1¹/₂ pounds crisp, fresh Swiss chard (preferably a mixture of red and green), woody ends discarded

1 tablespoon unsalted butter

¹/₂ teaspoon fine sea salt

Freshly ground black pepper

2 large eggs

¹/₄ cup crème fraîche

1 cup crumbled imported Roquefort cheese

¹/₄ cup snipped chives (¹/₂-inch lengths)

Bring a large pot of lightly salted water to a boil and preheat the oven to 425°F.

With kitchen shears, cut the leaves from the chard stems. Cut the stems into ¹/₂-inch pieces, and cut the leaves crosswise into 1-inch pieces. When the water is boiling briskly, add the stems, cook for 4 minutes, then add the leaves and cook for 1 minute more. Drain in a colander and rinse under cold water to stop the cooking. Press down hard to extract most of the water.

Place a large sauté pan over medium heat and add 1 tablespoon of the butter. When the butter has melted and is just beginning to turn brown, add all of the chard and cook, stirring occasionally, for about 4 minutes, until dry. Stir the salt and several grinds of pepper, and remove from the heat.

Generously butter a 10-inch round or 11 by 7-inch rectangular glass or ceramic baking dish. In a small bowl, whisk together the eggs and crème fraîche until smooth. Spread the chard in the baking dish and drizzle evenly with the crème fraîche mixture. Scatter with the Roquefort and half the chives and bake for 18 to 20 minutes, until the top is golden and the cheese is bubbling. Scatter with the remaining chives and let stand for 5 minutes before serving.

276 calories, 5 grams net carbs (8 grams less 3 grams fiber), 21 grams fat (13 grams saturated)

Wild Rice with Portobello Mushrooms and Hazelnuts

SERVES 4 * The Atkins diet made people afraid of all starch, but it's really just refined starches like white flour (including white bread and white pasta), white rice, and, of course, potatoes that you have to watch out for. Whole grains can be eaten in moderation, especially since their high fiber content helps to erase some of the carbohydrates. Here, as I often do, I've stretched the starch with mushrooms, making this dish particularly satisfying for the low-carbohydrate aficionado.

$3^1/_2$ ounces wild rice (about $^1/_2$ cup), rinsed

1 cup canned beef broth or water

1 cup veal demi-glace (see Note)

$^1/_2$ teaspoon fine sea salt and freshly ground black pepper

2 medium portobello mushrooms, brushed clean

Minced or grated zest of 1 large orange (about $1^1/_2$ teaspoons)

3 tablespoons unsalted butter, cut into 3 pieces

$^1/_3$ cup chopped hazelnuts

In a large saucepan, combine the wild rice, beef broth, veal demi-glace, and salt. Place over high heat and bring to a boil, then adjust the heat so that the liquid simmers very gently. Cover the pan and cook for 45 minutes, the rice should be not quite tender.

While the rice is simmering, discard the stems of the mushrooms and scrape away the brown gills with the edge of a spoon. Peel the mushrooms from the edges inward, just by pulling up on the skin, and chop coarsely. Stir the mushrooms, a few grinds of pepper, and about two thirds of the orange zest into the wild rice and cook, uncovered, stirring occasionally, for 5 to 10 minutes more, until the mushrooms are tender and the rice is done. Drain off any excess liquid in a colander and transfer the rice mixture to a covered serving bowl. Let stand in a low oven for 8 to 10 minutes.

After 5 minutes of standing time, place a small skillet over medium heat and add the butter. When the foam has subsided and the butter is beginning to brown, add the hazelnuts and sizzle for 2 to 3 minutes, until the butter is foamy and pale golden brown and the nuts are aromatic.

Drizzle the hazelnuts and all the butter over the wild rice, scatter with the remaining orange zest, and serve at once.

NOTE: Veal and poultry demi-glace (highly reduced broths) are available fresh or in the freezer section of many better supermarkets, and at www.vatelcuisine.com. Do not substitute one of the nonperishable products, which are made with starches, abundant salt, and preservatives.

204 calories, 15 grams net carbs (17 grams less 2 grams fiber), 14 grams fat (6 grams saturated)

Breakfast *and* Brunch

The egg is a versatile, nutritious, and, yes, healthy and miraculous little package.

DON'T EVEN THINK ABOUT FRENCH TOAST OR CROISSANTS. Find another vehicle for your butter.

Breakfast is a meal that many are tempted to skip (I certainly am), but it's the meal that sets you up for the day. Without early nourishment, your energy may flag in midmorning, and your brain won't work at top speed. But the low-carb devotee has some new thinking to adopt here. Orange juice, toast, bagels, French toast, hash browns, home fries, pancakes, waffles—all are simply out. What's left? Your friend the egg. But it won't be just scramble for the rest of your life; the egg is a versatile, nutritious, and, yes, healthy and miraculous little package. Think outside the box: An egg salad doesn't have to mean a slippery, white, and chunky concoction; it can become sunny-side-up eggs with baby greens and a fruity vinaigrette. Or, concoct a breakfast soufflé from traditional breakfast items: sausage, eggs, and spinach. For a quick breakfast, take a leaf out of the English book and broil some thick-sliced tomatoes and mushrooms to accompany an egg and a link of chicken sausage (skip the fried bread, please). Or add ricotta to extend the mixture for scrambled eggs.

For a little fruit on the side, choose fresh berries (the most low-carb-friendly fruit) with a dollop of crème fraîche and a sprinkle of nutmeg, or melon. Spinach is always a good breakfast choice, whether combined with eggs or not. It's full of vitamins and iron and is a good brain booster for the day.

There are two non-egg offerings in this chapter: the Tunisian-style breakfast *brik,* made from paper-thin phyllo and breakfast favorites smoked salmon, capers, chives, and cream cheese; and sweet little rice paper packets of apples and raspberries. If you get used to thinking outside the box on the breakfast issue, the possibilities open up.

Roast Chicken, Chard, and Sun-Dried Tomato Frittata

SERVES 6 ✳ Frittata is a dish that doesn't go out of style—ever. The low-carb lifestyle depends on frequent—and interesting—use of eggs, and the portability and sturdy nature of frittatas make them a natural for your new way of life. This frittata works well with rotisserie chicken from the market, with leftover roast chicken, or with any leftover meat, poultry, or even fish. The wedges are sturdy enough to be wrapped and packed for a picnic, especially after chilling.

1^1/$_2$ tablespoons olive or canola oil

1 medium leek, white and light green parts only, well washed and finely chopped

4 ounces Swiss chard, stems sliced ^{1}/$_4$ inch thick, leaves cut into 1-inch strips

2 large garlic cloves, minced or pressed

8 ounces diced roasted chicken (rotisserie chicken is perfect) or precooked chicken sausage (^{1}/$_4$-inch dice) (about 1^1/$_4$ cups)

2 tablespoons dry white wine

8 leaves fresh basil, julienned

5 sun-dried tomato halves, soaked in very hot water for 30 minutes, squeezed dry, and finely chopped

^{1}/$_2$ cup coarsely grated Pecorino Romano cheese

^{1}/$_2$ teaspoon fine sea salt

Freshly ground black pepper

7 large eggs

^{3}/$_4$ cup whole milk

1^1/$_2$ teaspoons Dijon mustard

Place an 8-inch oven-safe nonstick skillet over medium-low heat and add the oil. Add the leek and chard stems and sauté, stirring occasionally, for about 10 minutes, until tender. Add the chard leaves, cover the pan, and cook for about 5 minutes more, stirring once or twice, until wilted. Add the garlic and cook for 1 minute, then add the diced chicken and wine. Increase the heat to medium and simmer for 6 to 8 minutes, until the mixture is very dry. Remove the pan from the heat and stir in the basil, sun-dried tomatoes, Pecorino, salt, and a generous grinding of pepper. Stir well to distribute the ingredients in an even layer.

Preheat the broiler. In a bowl, thoroughly whisk together the eggs, milk, and mustard. Return the pan to medium-low heat and pour the egg mixture evenly over the ingredients. Cook without disturbing until the edges begin to set, 6 to 8 minutes. Pull one edge in gently and tilt the pan a little to let some of the uncooked egg run behind. Repeat in 2 or 3 other places around the rim as the eggs continue to set. When only the center is still wet and runny, transfer the pan to the broiler for 1 to 2 minutes, until set, firm, and golden. Turn off the broiler and let the frittata rest in the oven with the door open for 5 minutes. Loosen the sides with a small knife, place a plate upside down on top of the pan, and invert it, giving a brisk downward jerk to help release the frittata. Invert again onto another plate, so the golden side is uppermost. Cut into wedges and serve warm or at room temperature. The frittata can be refrigerated for up to 24 hours; return to room temperature before serving for the best flavor.

301 calories, 7 grams net carbs (8 grams less 1 gram fiber), 18 grams fat (6 grams saturated)

Smoked Salmon, Whipped Cream Cheese, and Red Onion Brik

SERVES 4 * In Tunisia a paper-thin dough known as *brik* (similar to the phyllo used here) is used to enclose vegetables, grapes, aromatics like herbs and spices, and eggs. I was searching for a way to serve the brunch favorites salmon, onion, capers, chives, and cream cheese without pizza dough, pumpernickel, or bagels, and this turned out to be a crisp and delicious alternative.

About $1/3$ cup unsalted butter, melted

5 ounces smoked salmon, coarsely chopped (trimmings are fine)

$1/4$ cup finely chopped red onion

1 cup whipped cream cheese, at room temperature

$1/8$ teaspoon fine sea salt

Freshly ground black pepper

2 tablespoons drained capers

2 tablespoons finely snipped chives

4 sheets completely thawed phyllo pastry (cover the pastry with a slightly damp towel to prevent it from drying out)

Preheat the oven to 400°F and brush a nonstick baking sheet with a little of the melted butter. In a bowl, combine the smoked salmon, red onion, cream cheese, salt, a few grinds of pepper, capers, and chives. Whisk with a fork until evenly mixed.

Place one sheet of phyllo pastry on a clean, dry surface, and brush one lengthwise half of the sheet with melted butter. Fold the pastry over itself to make a long, doubled sheet, and brush about 1 inch of all the outer edges with butter. Spread one quarter of the salmon mixture into a square shape at the short end of the sheet closest to you, leaving a $3/4$-inch border. Fold the packet upward, lining up the long edges, and brush the top with butter. Fold over once more, brush, and then fold in both sides of the remaining long edges all the way to the end. Continue folding and brushing until you reach the end, brush the top with butter, and place on the baking sheet. Make 3 more packets in the same way.

Bake for about 20 minutes, until golden and crisp; let rest for 5 minutes before serving.

370 calories, 11$1/2$ grams net carbs (12 grams less $1/2$ gram fiber), 33 grams fat (19 grams saturated)

Chicken-Apple Sausage, Spinach, and Gruyère Soufflé

SERVES 4 * Once you have perfected the very simple technique of making soufflés (see pages 64 and 98), here is another one for your low-carbohydrate recipe collection. It contains representatives from all the desirable breakfast food groups: light sausage, spinach, cheese, and eggs.

4 ounces (about 1 link) fresh chicken-apple sausage, casing removed

1¹/₂ tablespoons finely grated Parmesan cheese

1¹/₂ tablespoons unsalted butter

2 green onions, white and light green parts only, finely chopped

1 rounded tablespoon soy flour

1 cup whole milk

4 large eggs, at room temperature, separated, plus 2 additional egg whites

2 cups loosely packed baby spinach leaves (about 2 ounces), coarsely chopped

¹/₄ teaspoon plus a pinch of fine sea salt

White pepper, preferably freshly ground

¹/₂ cup grated Gruyère cheese

Place a nonstick or cast-iron skillet over medium-low heat and add the sausage meat. Cook, smashing, breaking up, and separating the sausage meat with a wooden spoon, until only just cooked through, with no trace of pink remaining, about 6 minutes. With a slotted spoon, transfer the sausage to a paper towel–lined plate and set aside.

Generously grease a 10-inch round, 11 by 7-inch, or similar-sized glass or ceramic gratin dish and sprinkle it with the Parmesan, shaking the dish so the cheese evenly coats the inside. Preheat the oven to 400°F and place the rack in the center of the oven.

In a large saucepan, heat the butter over medium-low heat. Add the green onions and stir for 2 minutes, then stir in the flour. Cook, stirring constantly, for 2 minutes, or until the butter and flour paste is frothy but not browned. Away from the heat, whisk in the milk. Return the pan to the heat and raise it to medium. Stir the mixture constantly with a wooden spoon until simmering and thickened, 5 to 10 minutes. Remove the pan from the heat and immediately add the egg yolks, one at a time, stirring each one in thoroughly. Thoroughly stir in the spinach, then stir in the sausage, ¹/₄ teaspoon salt, pepper, and cheese. Set aside.

In a large, clean bowl, using an electric mixer, beat the egg whites with a pinch of salt to firm peaks. Thoroughly stir one fourth of the egg whites into the sausage mixture to lighten it, then gently fold
in the remaining whites, being careful not to crush too much air out of them. The mixture should be only just combined. Turn into the prepared baking dish, place the dish on a baking sheet, and place in the oven. Reduce the temperature to 375°F and bake the soufflé for 20 minutes, until risen and golden. Serve immediately.

316 calories, 4¹/₂ grams net carbs (5 grams less ¹/₂ gram fiber), 23 grams fat (11 grams saturated)

Apple and Raspberry Crêpes with Nutmeg and Crème Fraîche

SERVES 4 ✳ Fruit is shunned by the Atkins regime, but the South Beach diet allows some fruit, and I have to agree. Berries and melon are the best choices, and apples in moderation provide flavor, sweetness, and, of course, much-needed fiber. These little crêpes, made from rice paper—which crisps nicely when brushed with butter and baked—should be seen as a breakfast side, not a main feature. They are small, satisfying, and full of flavor and would make a fine accompaniment to scrambled eggs and crisped Canadian bacon (which has less fat than standard bacon), shirred eggs, or a frittata.

1 medium cooking apple, peeled, cored, and finely chopped

2 teaspoons granular Splenda

1 teaspoon minced or grated orange zest

1/2 teaspoon ground nutmeg, plus more for serving

1 1/2 tablespoons plus 1/4 cup crème fraîche

1/2 cup plus 1/4 cup fresh raspberries, wiped clean

4 circles medium rice paper (8 5/8 inch diameter)

2 tablespoons unsalted butter, melted

In a bowl, combine the apple, Splenda, orange zest, nutmeg, and 1 1/2 tablespoons of the crème fraîche. Fold in 1/2 cup raspberries.

Preheat the oven to 400°F.

Fill a large bowl with hot water. Gently working with 1 sheet of rice paper at a time, dip the paper into the water completely for 2 seconds. Place on a damp kitchen towel (the rice paper should become pliable within moments). Brush the rice paper all over with melted butter and place one fourth of the filling in the center of the bottom half, leaving a 1 1/2-inch border along the bottom edge. Fold up the bottom edge of the paper, then fold in the sides. Brush the unbuttered sides of the rice paper with melted butter, then roll the rice paper up from the bottom into a compact cylinder. Brush the top of the roll all over with butter, and place, seam side up, on a nonstick baking sheet. Make the remaining 3 rolls in the same way.

Bake the crêpes until golden brown and crispy, about 18 minutes. Place a crêpe on each serving plate and sprinkle with a little nutmeg. Place a spoonful of crème fraîche on one side, nestle a few raspberries in the crème fraîche, and serve warm.

196 calories, 17 grams net carbs (19 grams less 2 grams fiber), 12 grams fat (8 grams saturated)

Baby Greens and Pink Grapefruit on a Bed of Sunny-Side-Up Eggs

SERVES 4 ✳ Many of the dishes in this book have been part of my repertoire for years, some in a different, carbohydrate-rich form, some just the way they are. But this is a dish I invented after embracing the low-carb lifestyle, and it sums up everything I like about the regime. The salad is crisp and the grapefruit juicy, the dressing has an element of fruit flavor and a bracing brightness from the vinegar, and the eggs are satisfying, runny, and rich. Not only is this a great breakfast dish, but on those "pajamas-at-seven" nights that all girls need periodically, this is my menu of choice.

1 pink grapefruit

1¹/₂ tablespoons raspberry vinegar

1 tablespoon mild (domestic) Dijon mustard

¹/₄ teaspoon fine sea salt, plus more to taste

Freshly ground black pepper

3 tablespoons hazelnut or walnut oil

2 tablespoons canola oil

2 tablespoons unsalted butter

8 large free-range eggs

4 cups baby salad greens, including frisée, washed and dried

Cut off the top and bottom of the grapefruit with a sharp knife, revealing the flesh. Stand the grapefruit upright and trim off the peel and all the pith, cutting down to, but not too far into, the flesh. Turn the grapefruit as you trim, then turn it over and trim off the rest of the peel and pith. Working over a bowl, carefully cut between the membranes to release each segment (called a suprème). Cut the segments into ¹/₄-inch dice and reserve with the juices.

In a large mixing bowl, combine the vinegar, mustard, ¹/₄ teaspoon salt, several turns of the peppermill, hazelnut oil, and canola oil. Whisk energetically until creamy, and set aside.

Warm 4 plates in a low oven. Place a very large nonstick pan over medium heat and add the butter (or use 2 pans with 1¹/₂ tablespoons of butter in each one). When the foam has subsided, carefully break the eggs just above the hot surface of the pan. Immediately reduce the heat to very low and cover the pan tightly. Cook slowly until the whites are firm and the yolks have begun to thicken but are not hard, about 3 minutes. If desired, baste the tops of the yolks with a little butter by tilting the pan and spooning up the pooled butter from the edge. You can carefully salt the whites, but do not salt the yolks, or the salt will mar the perfect yellow orbs.

About a minute before the eggs will be done, add the salad greens to the bowl containing the vinaigrette and toss thoroughly. Slide 2 eggs onto each plate and, with tongs, place a nice mound of the salad on top. Scatter the grapefruit segments over the salad, drizzle with the remaining grapefruit juice, and serve at once.

384 calories, 6 grams net carbs (8 grams less 2 grams fiber), 33 grams fat (8 grams saturated)

Shirred Eggs *on a* Bed *of* Spinach *with* Roasted Peppers

SERVES 4 * Another exciting, vegetable-rich option for serving your new best friend, the egg. Eggs from free-range, organically or sprout-fed chickens are a good investment when the egg becomes a prominent feature in your diet: the yolks are a lovely rich yellow (not like the insipid, pale yolks of the usual supermarket eggs), and they have a richer, more complex flavor. For many years I thought shirred eggs terribly old-fashioned, but after writing a breakfast cookbook I learned to love them.

1 red bell pepper, washed

3^1/$_2$ pounds fresh spinach, stemmed and well washed (about 1 ^{3}/$_4$ pounds stemless leaves)

1 tablespoon unsalted butter

^{1}/$_2$ cup heavy whipping cream

^{1}/$_2$ teaspoon fine sea salt

Freshly ground black pepper

Pinch of ground nutmeg

4 extra-large or jumbo eggs, preferably free-range

Roast the pepper over a gas flame, turning it with tongs, until the skin is blistered and blackened (but not ashy) all over. Put the pepper into a brown paper bag and twist the top closed. Let stand for 10 to 15 minutes, then remove the pepper and slide the skin off with your fingers or a clean towel (holding the pepper under cold running water makes the job easier, but sacrifices flavor). Cut around and remove the stem, then cut down one side of the pepper and open it out flat. Cut lengthwise into ^{1}/$_4$-inch strips and set aside.

Bring a large saucepan of lightly salted water to a boil and add the spinach. Make sure it is all submerged and cook for 2 minutes, then immediately drain in a colander and run under copious amounts of cold running water until no longer warm. Gather the spinach into balls and squeeze very firmly to extract as much water as possible. Chop coarsely.

In a large skillet, melt the butter over medium heat. Add the spinach and cook, stirring frequently, until any excess moisture has evaporated, about 4 minutes. (The spinach should not brown.) Stir in the cream, salt, a generous grinding of black pepper, and the nutmeg and cook for 4 minutes more, until thick and quite dry. Remove from the heat.

Preheat the oven to 350°F and generously butter 4 small, round, shallow individual gratin dishes. Divide the spinach among the dishes and smooth the top into a perfectly even surface. With the back of a large tablespoon, form a rounded 1¹/₂-inch depression in the top of the spinach in each dish. Break an egg into each depression. Carefully transfer the dishes to the oven and bake for 10 to 12 minutes, until the whites of the eggs are set and the yolks are still distinctly runny (they will continue to cook after coming out of the oven).

Remove from the oven, drape a few strips of red pepper around each egg, and serve at once.

272 calories, 4 grams net carbs (10 grams less 6 grams fiber), 21 grams fat (11 grams saturated)

Fish and Shellfish

Everything about fish is right for the low-carbohydrate regime: It is high in protein, low in saturated fat, and contains hardly any carbohydrates.

MOST DIETARY REGIMENS INVOLVE some sort of deprivation, I think we can all agree. It's true that you may miss bread, potatoes, and pasta at first. Soon, however, the repertoire of vegetables, poultry, and, of course, fish and shellfish will be all you will crave. There is comforting, fireside-dining fish like Seared Scallops and Caramelized Cauliflower Florets with Salsa Verde (page 93), and there is fancy, impress-your-friends fish like Dungeness Crab and Fennel Salad with Ginger-Curry Aïoli (page 90). In between are sashimi-grade tuna and yellowtail from your local Japanese market, steamed salmon (make a simple mayonnaise-y sauce), and whole, steamed lobsters that you might serve with lemon-scented drawn butter at a summer pool party. Every step of the way, you'll be doing your body—not just your taste buds—a truly loving favor.

Everything about fish is right for the low-carbohydrate regime: It is high in protein, low in saturated fat, and contains hardly any carbohydrates. You can pair it, in moderation of course, with butter and cream, or with assertive and rustic flavors like olives, parsley, and grapefruit. When escorted by the appropriate herbs and spices—say, tarragon or curry—fish comes alive with flavor. And alive is what it should just recently have been, of course. Many books explain how to judge fresh fish, but I will emphasize the importance of high quality in this perishable and pure foodstuff. In fact, why not select every food that you put into your body with the care and respect you both deserve? Did the cream come from a local dairy? Is the butter the best you can buy? How about the tuna? Is it shiny with freshness, pink and juicy? Take the time to search out the good ingredients, and remember that not only do you deserve the best treatment, but they do as well.

Pepper-Crusted Soft-Shell Crabs
with Grapefruit Beurre Blanc

SERVES 6 * Frying soft-shell crabs without bread crumbs produces a tasty but disappointing dish, lacking the spectacular crunch that I expect from these little crustaceans (which should be bought alive and must be served the same day). I'm not much of a pork-rind gal, but legions of Internet low-carb forums couldn't be wrong, so I gave it a try here as a substitute for bread crumbs, and was thrilled with the results. I got the crunch, and there's not a hint of porky flavor (perhaps because I spiced up the coating mixture so much).

To cut grapefruit into perfect, pithless dice, halve and then peel the grapefruit down to the flesh with a sharp knife, removing all the white pith. Remove the segments by cutting carefully between the membranes, to yield suprèmes. Cut the suprèmes into tiny dice. For frying the crabs, I recommend nonstick skillets; if none are available, use a sturdy metal spatula to turn the crabs and make sure none of the delicious crust is left behind in the pan. Note that for hungry diners, you may want to serve two crabs per person. This will not affect the carbohydrate or fat count, but you will probably need to cook the crabs in batches, to avoid overcrowding the pans.

COATING

2 ounces puffed pork rinds, available in the snack and chip section of many supermarkets

2 tablespoons sweet paprika

2 bay leaves, crushed

1 1/2 teaspoons coarse sea salt

1 teaspoon freshly ground black pepper

3/4 teaspoon togarashi pepper blend (see Note)

3/4 teaspoon dried thyme

1/2 cup white wine, such as a fruity sauvignon blanc

1/4 cup dry vermouth

1 tablespoon white wine vinegar

1 large shallot, finely chopped

To prepare the coating, in a food processor, process the pork rinds in several batches, to the consistency of fine bread crumbs. Transfer to a plate, then combine the paprika, bay leaves, salt, black pepper, togarashi, and thyme in the processor. Process for 1 minute (make sure the bay leaves are broken up), then add to the pork rinds and blend together evenly with a fork. Set aside.

In a small saucepan, combine the wine, vermouth, vinegar, and shallot and place over medium-high heat. Bring to a boil, then reduce the heat to low. Simmer gently until reduced to about 1 tablespoon, watching carefully, about 15 minutes. Set aside.

To prepare the watercress salad, in a large bowl, whisk together the vinegar, 1/8 teaspoon salt, a pinch of pepper, and the olive oil until smooth. Add the watercress and the shallot and toss to combine and coat evenly. Set aside.

Clean the crabs by snipping off their "faces" with kitchen shears, pulling away the flap from underneath, and removing the spongy gills. Rinse under cool running water and pat dry thoroughly with paper towels.

continued

WATERCRESS SALAD

1 tablespoon white wine vinegar

$^1/_8$ teaspoon fine sea salt

Pinch of white pepper, preferably freshly ground

2$^1/_2$ tablespoons extra virgin olive oil

3 small bunches watercress, tough stems removed, washed and spun dry

1 shallot, finely chopped

6 soft-shell crabs, alive or very recently alive

6 tablespoons (3 ounces) unsalted butter, at room temperature, cut into $^1/_2$-inch cubes

1$^1/_2$ cups diced fresh pink or white grapefruit ($^1/_4$-inch dice; about 1 grapefruit)

2 tablespoons finely snipped chives

1 cup canola or vegetable oil

$^3/_4$ cup heavy whipping cream

Place the saucepan containing the wine-shallot mixture over low heat, to warm. As soon as it is steaming, add all the butter at once and swirl the pan or whisk the sauce continuously until the butter melts and the sauce emulsifies. Remove from the heat, add the grapefruit and chives and swirl again. Cover the pan and set aside at the back of the stove, off the heat. Proceed immediately to frying the crabs.

Place 2 large skillets over medium-high heat and add half a cup of the oil to each pan. Place the cream in a shallow bowl near the stovetop with the plate of coating mixture next to it. When the oil is hot but not smoking, quickly dip both sides of the crabs in the cream and then dredge them through the coating mixture, pressing to help it adhere.

Carefully slide 3 of the crabs into each hot pan and sauté without disturbing for 4 minutes. Turn and sauté for 4 minutes more, until golden and crisp. Transfer to folded paper towels for a moment or two to remove excess oil, and place a crab on each of 6 warmed dinner plates. Top with a large spoonful of the sauce and place a mound of the watercress salad on the top.

NOTE: Togarashi pepper is a Japanese blend that is available in Asian markets and from gourmet websites. Lemon pepper or any coarsely ground pepper blend can be substituted.

428 calories, 5 grams net carbs (6 grams less 1 gram fiber), 32 grams fat (16 grams saturated)

Dungeness Crab and Fennel Salad
with Ginger-Curry Aïoli

SERVES 4 * At some point in my teenage years I remember a day when my mother (a California native) announced with glee, "The Dungeness are back!" (For various reasons there had, at that time, been no harvest of Dungeness crabs for about fifteen years.) Now we've become jaded to the availability of this richly flavored and superior crabmeat. It might be wise to keep in mind that in our uncertain and careless world, it could easily disappear again. This is an exceedingly stylish and very pretty dish, one that is worthy of a really good French white burgundy or California chardonnay and your best china. It could be a brunch or lunch dish, or a main course for a summer evening. You can make a ring for forming the salads by removing the top and bottom from an empty tuna can.

1 bulb fennel, quartered lengthwise and trimmed of stalks and any discolored areas

12 ounces fresh Dungeness crabmeat, picked over for bits of shell and pulled apart into nice chunks (do not shred)

1 medium shallot, minced

2 stalks celery, strings removed, cut into $1/8$-inch dice

2 tablespoons finely snipped chives

2 tablespoons finely chopped flat-leaf parsley

$1/2$ cup Aïoli-Mayo Base (page 150) or store-bought mayonnaise

$1^1/2$ tablespoons fresh lemon juice

$1^1/2$ teaspoons grated fresh ginger and juice, or ginger paste (see Note)

$1/4$ teaspoon best-quality curry powder

$1/2$ teaspoon fine sea salt, plus more to taste

Freshly ground black pepper

Trim away most of the fennel's core in a triangular wedge, leaving just enough to hold it together. With a very sharp knife, slice the fennel crosswise as thinly as possible (it should be almost paper-thin). Chop finely.

In a mixing bowl, combine the fennel, crab, shallot, celery, chives, and parsley. Add the aioli-mayo base, lemon juice, ginger, curry powder, salt, and a few grinds of pepper. Mix together with a fork until evenly blended, but don't blend so much that you break up all the little lumps of crabmeat. Taste for seasoning. If desired, cover and refrigerate the salad for up to 4 hours. Let stand at room temperature for 10 minutes before serving.

Chill 4 plates.

Arrange half an avocado on each plate in a flower shape, about 6 inches wide, with the rounded sides out and a hole in the center. Place a $3^1/4$-inch round cookie cutter on a wide spatula and pack one fourth of the crab salad firmly into it, smoothing the top. Slide the salad out into the center of the avocado flower and ease the cookie cutter up and off. Repeat with the remaining salad. Scatter the grapefruit dice on top of each crab disk, and place a pinched mound of sprouts on the top.

2 avocados, pitted, peeled, and thinly sliced crosswise

1 grapefruit, peeled, cut into segments (see page 80), and diced, saving the juice

1 cup loosely packed alfalfa sprouts, for garnish

2 tablespoon drained capers, for garnish

Extra virgin olive oil, for drizzling

Scatter the capers around the edges of the plates, and drizzle the edges with the reserved grapefruit juice and a little extra virgin olive oil. Serve at once.

NOTE: Japanese supermarkets and websites carry tubes of ginger paste, which are indispensable for the busy cook. After you open it, the paste will last for several months in the refrigerator, and it tastes virtually the same as grated fresh ginger.

480 calories, 11 grams net carbs (18 grams less 7 grams fiber), 38 grams fat (6 grams saturated)

Vietnamese Salad *on* Sushi-Grade Yellowtail

SERVES 4 ＊ I've been fascinated by Vietnamese cuisine for some years now, seduced by the abundant use of fresh herbs, the insistence on fresh ingredients, and the light and clean flavors. In this dish the sharp and perky flavors of the herbs add a unique element to what is essentially sashimi (sushi without the rice). To me, the flavors are far more interesting than a piece of fresh yellowtail perched on a wedge of rice. Note that fish sauce should be appreciated only for its ability to complement the flavor of other ingredients—it should never be smelled straight from the bottle!

DRESSING

1 very small, very hot chile such as serrano or bird's eye

3 tablespoons Thai or Vietnamese fish sauce

3 tablespoons Japanese rice vinegar

1 tablespoon extra virgin olive oil

1 teaspoon tamari or soy sauce

1 clove garlic, minced or pressed

1 tablespoon granular Splenda

2 cups loosely packed cilantro leaves, washed, spun dry, and kept chilled

1 cup loosely packed mint leaves, washed, spun dry, and kept chilled

6 ounces bean sprouts

4 large shiso (ohba) leaves (see Notes), cut into 1/4-inch chiffonade

3 green onions, crisp green parts only, finely sliced

2 tablespoons minced red bell pepper (optional, for color)

1 1/4 pounds sushi-grade yellowtail (hamachi), sliced 1/4 inch thick with a very sharp knife and kept very cold

1/2 cup dry-roasted salted pecans

To prepare the dressing, stem and seed the chile, quarter lengthwise, and shred finely. In a large mixing bowl, combine the fish sauce, rice vinegar, olive oil, soy sauce, chile, garlic, and Splenda, and whisk to blend. Set aside (whisk again just before adding the herbs). Chill 4 dinner plates.

Just before serving, whisk the dressing again and add the cilantro, mint, bean sprouts, shiso, green onions, and red bell pepper to the bowl. Toss gently to coat the ingredients evenly.

Divide the sliced yellowtail among the 4 plates, fanning the fish out in an even layer. With tongs, top the yellowtail with a tall mound of salad and scatter the pecans over the top. Serve at once.

NOTES: When working with searingly hot peppers like these, wear surgical gloves or afterwards wash your hands repeatedly in hot, soapy water. The volatile oils are no joke; should they come into contact with any mucous membrane, you will be in agony.

Shiso is an herb from the mint family with hints of basil and spearmint. It is now widely available in Japanese markets and where sushi is sold; if unavailable, substitute basil.

365 calories, 6 grams net carbs (8 grams less 2 grams fiber), 11 grams fat (2 grams saturated)

Seared Scallops *and* Caramelized Cauliflower Florets *with* Salsa Verde

SERVES 4 * Earthy, Provençal-style flavors dominate and richly perfume this rustic dish—it's not the creamy, delicate scallop presentation that your mother might have served in a little shell-shaped dish. For a brighter flavor in the sauce, substitute a cup of fresh mint leaves for 1 cup of the parsley. In any case, be sure to remove all the stems for the smoothest result. If you do not have two large, well-seasoned cast-iron skillets, substitute a heavy-bottomed cast aluminum skillet for one or both pans. If the scallops threaten to stick to the pan, release them with the edge of a metal spatula before gently turning them over with tongs—the crust is a crucial part of this dish.

SALSA VERDE

4 cups loosely packed flat-leaf parsley leaves (about 2 ounces), washed and spun dry

2 oil- or salt-packed anchovy fillets (salt-packed anchovies are packed whole; halve lengthwise to yield 2 fillets)

3 cloves garlic, minced or pressed

1 tablespoon drained capers

2 tablespoons Dijon mustard

1 tablespoon white wine vinegar

$1/4$ teaspoon fine sea salt

Freshly ground black pepper

$2/3$ cup extra virgin olive oil

1 tablespoon water

1 small head cauliflower, about $1^{1}/2$ pounds, separated into 1-inch florets with about $3/4$ inch of stem attached

Fine sea salt and freshly ground black pepper

2 teaspoons olive or canola oil

To prepare the salsa, in a food processor, combine the parsley, anchovies, garlic, capers, mustard, vinegar, salt, and several turns of the peppermill. Pulse several times to combine and, with the motor running, add the olive oil in a thin stream and continue processing until smooth and creamy. Add the water to loosen the mixture slightly. If desired, cover and refrigerate the salsa for up to 2 hours before serving (any longer and, though the flavor will still be good, the bright color of the parsley will turn dull). Return to room temperature for 20 minutes, if chilled.

In the top of a covered steamer over simmering water, steam the cauliflower florets until tender, 5 to 10 minutes. Remove from the steamer and let stand on a paper towel–lined plate until serving time.

Warm 4 dinner plates and a platter in a low oven.

Season the cauliflower florets and the scallops generously on both sides with salt and pepper. Place 2 large, well-seasoned cast-iron skillets over medium-high heat and add half the oil and butter to each one. When the pans are hot, add half the cauliflower florets to each and sear until golden brown, pressing down on them gently with the back of a spatula to bring more of the floret into contact with the hot pan. Turn over and sear until brown on the other side. Transfer the cauliflower to the warm platter and carefully place half the scallops in each pan, without crowding them. Sear without moving or touching for 2 minutes, then turn over with tongs and sear for 2 to $2^{1}/2$ minutes more, until only just barely translucent in a thin band around the center.

continued

2 teaspoons unsalted butter

12 large dry-packed diver-caught scallops, patted dry with paper towels

4 teaspoons warm, slightly reduced balsamic vinegar (see Note)

Flood one side of each plate with $^1/_4$ cup of the salsa verde and place 3 scallops on top of the sauce. Divide the cauliflower among the plates, arranging it across from the scallops, and drizzle the cauliflower with the balsamic syrup. Serve at once.

NOTE: To reduce balsamic vinegar to a syrupy consistency, perfect for drizzling, gently simmer $^1/_2$ cup vinegar in a small saucepan until thickened. When cool, the syrup will be almost solid; warm it gently to achieve a flowing consistency. The syrup will keep almost indefinitely at room temperature; leave it in a small saucepan—like a butter warmer—until needed.

123 calories, 6 grams net carbs (10 grams less 4 grams fiber), 6 grams fat (2 grams saturated)

Pan-Roasted Sea Bass *with* Truffle-Leek Nage Sauce

SERVES 4 ∗ I first became aware of *nage* sauces when writing Joachim Splichal's *Patina Cookbook: Spuds, Truffles, and Wild Gnocchi*. A *nage* is thickened entirely in the blender by forming an emulsion between a vegetable stock and cold butter. Here, the *nage* enters distinctly grand territory with the addition of cream and truffle oil. It's a very rich sauce, and I suggest you supply soup spoons because there is usually a lot of somewhat uncivilized slurping when this dish is served. Although I normally warm plates and bowls in the oven, in this case a hot bowl would cause the delicate sauce to break.

This is another trés soigné dish that deserves the best complex and buttery white wine you can afford, and a beautifully set table.

10 tablespoons (5 ounces) very cold unsalted butter, cut into about 20 pieces

2 leeks, white and light green parts only, well washed and coarsely chopped

1 small onion, coarsely chopped

2 stalks celery, coarsely chopped

1 sprig fresh thyme

1 sprig fresh rosemary

1 bay leaf

2 tablespoons black peppercorns

1 cup dry white wine

4 cups water

1¹/₂ pounds sea bass or other whitefish, cut into 4 equal pieces and patted dry with paper towels

Put the pieces of butter on a small plate and place it in the freezer.

In a large saucepan, combine the leeks, onion, celery, thyme, rosemary, bay leaf, and peppercorns. Add the wine, cover the pan, and place over medium heat. Bring to a simmer and cook for 10 minutes. Add the water, return to a slow simmer, and cook for 20 minutes more. Remove from the heat and strain the broth into another saucepan, pressing down on the solids. Over high heat, simmer the sauce briskly until reduced by three quarters, to about 1 cup of liquid, 20 to 25 minutes. Cover the pan and set aside until just before serving time.

Preheat the oven to 350°F. Season both sides of the sea bass generously with salt and pepper.

Place a large, oven-safe sauté pan over medium-high heat and add the canola oil and butter. When the pan is very hot and the foam has subsided, add the sea bass and sear for 2 minutes without disturbing. Carefully turn over and sear for 1¹/₂ minutes more.

Fine sea salt and white pepper, preferably freshly ground

2 teaspoons canola oil

2 teaspoons unsalted butter

$^{1}/_{4}$ cup heavy whipping cream

2 tablespoons white truffle oil

$^{1}/_{2}$ teaspoon grated or minced lemon zest

2 teaspoons finely snipped chives, for garnish

20 asparagus tips, blanched until crisp-tender but still bright green, drained and warmed in a little butter, for serving (optional)

Transfer the pan to the oven to finish cooking for 10 to 12 minutes, until firm and just opaque through to the center. While the fish is roasting, return the vegetable stock to a low simmer and stir in the heavy cream and a pinch of salt and pepper. Simmer for 1 minute, then transfer to a blender and add the truffle oil, lemon zest, and cold butter.

Blend at high speed until smooth and foamy. Divide the thin sauce among 4 large, shallow bowls and place a piece of sea bass in the center of each. Scatter with chives. If using, place the asparagus tips in a little mound on one side of the plate and serve at once, with spoons for slurping up the delicious sauce.

645 calories, 3 grams net carbs (4 grams less 1 gram fiber), 47 grams fat (23 grams saturated)

Crayfish Soufflé *with* Tarragon Sabayon

SERVES 4 TO 6 * In the eighties, I spent a few years living in a large Tudor house about an hour south of London. The day before moving out, I threw a blowout Sunday lunch at which this sophisticated soufflé was the star starter. One of the benefits of country living, at least there in Hampshire, was a crayfish farm about ten miles away, and I duly placed my order a week in advance. When I arrived however, only a few crawlers were to be seen in the tank. So off we went in a rowboat to pull in a few pots and fill my order. It doesn't get any fresher.

TARRAGON SABAYON

3 large egg yolks

$^2/_3$ cup Riesling wine or vermouth

1 teaspoon brandy or Cognac

$^1/_4$ teaspoon fine sea salt

Pinch of white pepper, preferably freshly ground

Freshly grated Parmesan cheese, for preparing the gratin dish

3 tablespoons unsalted butter

1 shallot, very finely chopped

2 tablespoons all-purpose flour

$^3/_4$ cup whole milk

$^1/_2$ cup rich lobster stock (see Note)

$^1/_4$ cup heavy whipping cream

$^1/_3$ cup grated Gruyère cheese

5 large eggs, separated, plus 1 additional egg white (have the whites at room temperature)

To prepare the sabayon, place a large bowl over a large saucepan containing about 2 inches of warm water to form a double boiler (be sure the base of the bowl is not touching the water). In the bowl, combine the egg yolks, wine, brandy, salt, and pepper. Set aside at the back of the stove off the heat, while you begin the soufflé.

Preheat the oven to 400°F. Butter a 10-cup (2 liter) capacity or similar-sized gratin dish and dust the inside with Parmesan, shaking it to coat the base and sides evenly, and tipping out any excess.

In a large saucepan, heat the butter over medium-low heat. Add the shallot and stir for 3 minutes, then stir in the flour, stirring until a loose paste forms. Cook, stirring constantly, for 2 to 3 minutes, or until the paste is smooth and frothy but not browned. Remove the pan from the heat and whisk in the milk, lobster stock, and cream. Return the pan to the stove and increase the heat to medium. Stir the mixture constantly with a wooden spoon until gently simmering and quite thick, about 5 minutes. Remove from the heat and stir in the Gruyère, then add the egg yolks one at a time, stirring well immediately after you add the first one. Stir in the salt, white pepper, nutmeg, and the chopped crayfish.

In a large, perfectly clean bowl, beat the 6 egg whites until foamy, then add the lemon juice and a tiny pinch of salt and continue beating until stiff—but not grainy—peaks form. Stir about a quarter of the egg whites into the crayfish mixture to lighten it. Using a large rubber spatula, gently fold the crayfish mixture into the bowl of remaining whites with a gentle, scooping, up-and-over motion, taking care not to stir too much air out of the mixture. It should be only just combined. Gently scoop into the prepared

¹/₂ teaspoon fine sea salt

Pinch of white pepper, preferably freshly ground

Pinch of ground nutmeg

6 ounces cooked crayfish meat, finely chopped (crab or shrimp may be substituted)

¹/₄ teaspoon fresh lemon juice

2 teaspoons minced fresh tarragon leaves

baking dish and place in the oven. Immediately reduce the temperature to 375°F and bake the soufflé for about 25 minutes, until puffed about 1¹/₂ inches above the rim and golden brown.

While the soufflé is baking, remove the bowl from the top of the saucepan and bring the water in the pan to a simmer. Reduce the heat so the water is just barely simmering. In the bowl, beat the yolk and wine mixture with a hand-held electric mixer set to low speed until smooth, then place the bowl over the hot water. Whisk constantly for about 5 minutes, until the mixture is light and frothy and doubled in volume (keep checking the water underneath, to make sure it does not begin to boil). Remove the bowl from the saucepan and beat for 15 seconds more to stabilize the foam. Fold in the tarragon, and serve the foamy sauce within 5 minutes (after this it will begin to separate).

As soon as the soufflé is done, serve it immediately in large spoonfuls. Drizzle the warm sabayon around the edge of the plates.

NOTE: Lobster stock is available in the freezer section of many fish markets and better supermarkets, and at www.vatelcuisine.com. Substitute a rich fish stock if unavailable.

For 4: 361 calories, 7 grams net carbs (7 grams less 0 grams fiber), 24 grams fat (12 grams saturated)

For 6: 240 calories, 5 grams net carbs (5 grams less 0 grams fiber), 16 grams fat (8 grams saturated)

Salmon Burgers *with* Pinot Noir Glaze *and* Pancetta Chips

SERVES 4 * The partnership of salmon and red wine has become one of those lyrical, legendary pairings, like tomatoes and basil, Champagne and caviar, or warm sourdough bread and French butter (well, once in a while). The tannins of the wine serve to cut the fattiness of the salmon to just the right degree, without overwhelming the flavor, while conversely, a more delicate sauce would be overwhelmed by the salmon's own assertive flavor. I've always liked to serve a little cured pork with fish. Here, crisp pancetta disks replace the bun on this light but sophisticated "burger."

1¹/₂ pounds fresh wild salmon, bones and skin removed

2 shallots, very finely chopped

Finely grated zest of 1 lime

2 teaspoons grated fresh ginger and juice, or ginger paste (see Notes)

3 tablespoons cottage cheese

2 large egg yolks, lightly beaten

¹/₂ teaspoon fine sea salt

Pinch of freshly ground black pepper

4 slices pancetta, ¹/₈ inch thick (thicker than pancetta is normally cut; ask your deli counter)

PINOT NOIR GLAZE

2 tablespoons unsalted butter, cut into 2 pieces

Half a small onion, finely chopped

2 cloves garlic, sliced

¹/₄ cup tomato juice

2 cups pinot noir or other fruity red wine, such as zinfandel

Cut the salmon into scant ¹/₄-inch dice and, in a bowl, combine with the shallots, lime zest, ginger, cottage cheese, egg yolks, salt, and pepper. Mix together well and shape into 4 loose, rounded patties (handle the patties as little as possible). Transfer to a parchment paper–lined platter, cover, and refrigerate for at least 1 hour and up to 2 hours before cooking.

Preheat the oven to 300°F. Place the pancetta on a parchment-lined baking sheet and top with another sheet of parchment and a baking sheet that is the same size or that will sit flat on top of the paper. Bake for 45 to 50 minutes, until golden brown and crisp. Transfer to paper towels and set aside until serving time. (Begin the glaze while the chips are cooking, if desired.)

To prepare the glaze, place a saucepan over medium-low heat and add the butter. Sauté the onion and garlic until softened, about 4 minutes. Add the tomato juice and pinot noir and adjust the heat so the liquid simmers briskly. Reduce by about three fourths, until about ¹/₂ cup of liquid remains, 15 to 20 minutes. Strain into a small, clean saucepan, pressing hard on the solids, and stir in the veal demi-glace. Simmer until reduced by about half, to ¹/₂ cup or so of very thick and syrupy liquid. Season with the salt and pepper and remove from the heat. Cover and let stand until serving time.

Place a large, nonstick skillet over medium-high heat and add the butter. When the foam has subsided, add the burgers to the pan carefully, sliding them off the end of a wide spatula. Do not attempt to move them until they have cooked for at least 1 minute; this will allow the patties to "seize" so they will not fall apart when

continued

1 cup veal or poultry demi-glace (canned broth or consommé will not work here; see Notes)

$^1/_4$ teaspoon fine sea salt

Pinch of freshly ground black pepper

$1^1/_2$ tablespoon unsalted butter

you turn them. (Fry in two batches if necessary—do not overcrowd the pan; there should be 1 inch clearance between the burgers.) Fry until crisp and golden on the outside but still moist within, about $2^1/_2$ minutes on each side.

Warm the reserved sauce until steaming.

Place a burger on each plate and drizzle a little of the very thick and intense sauce over each one. Top with a pancetta chip, and serve at once.

NOTES: Japanese supermarkets and websites carry tubes of ginger paste, which are indispensable for the busy cook. After you open it, the paste will last for several months in the refrigerator, and it tastes virtually the same as grated fresh ginger.

Veal and poultry demi-glace (highly reduced stocks) are available fresh or in the freezer section of many better supermarkets, and at www.vatelcuisine.com. Do not substitute one of the nonperishable products, which are made with starches, abundant salt, and preservatives.

564 calories, 6 grams net carbs (7 grams less 1 gram fiber),
33 grams fat (13 grams saturated)

Hazelnut-Crusted Freshwater Trout *with* Preserved Lemon Relish

SERVES 4 * In my *Polenta* book there is a cornmeal-crusted trout that tasted fantastic and looked very nice when I made it, but ended up looking like an unnatural cardboard cutout in the photo (it's bothered me ever since). Here is my modern version, accompanied by a salty-gingery-sour relish that also makes a very nice base for vinaigrette. Preserved lemons are available in some gourmet markets; you can make the traditional 2-week version or the quick 4-day version (pages 151, 152). Nuts have heart-healthy oils, and here they make a better-than-the original substitute for bread crumbs.

PRESERVED LEMON RELISH

About ²/₃ cup coarsely chopped preserved lemon zest (from 3 preserved lemons, see page 151), rinsed well, drained, and patted dry

¹/₂ cup brine-cured green olives such as picholine, pitted

2¹/₂ teaspoons ground ginger

¹/₂ teaspoon ground coriander

¹/₄ teaspoon ground turmeric

¹/₄ teaspoon ground cinnamon

1 to 2 teaspoons olive or canola oil

2 large whole trout (about 1¹/₂ pounds each), cleaned, boned, and butterflied (about 12 ounces each after cleaning)

¹/₂ cup whole hazelnuts (filberts), very finely chopped

¹/₃ cup finely grated Italian fontina, jack, or havarti cheese

2 teaspoons finely chopped flat-leaf parsley

2 teaspoons finely chopped fresh mint

¹/₂ teaspoon fine sea salt

Freshly ground black pepper

To prepare the relish, in a food processor, combine the lemon zest, olives, ginger, coriander, turmeric, and cinnamon. Pulse briefly just a few times, scraping down the sides, to make a chunky paste; do not overprocess. Transfer to a bowl and stir in just enough olive oil to bind the mixture. Set aside at room temperature for at least 1 and up to 4 hours, for the flavors to marry and mellow. If desired, refrigerate for up to 1 week. Return to room temperature for 30 minutes before serving.

Preheat the oven to 450°F. Pat the trout dry gently with paper towels. In a bowl, combine the hazelnuts, cheese, parsley, mint, salt, and a few turns of the peppermill and toss to mix evenly. Place the trout fillets skin side down in a well-oiled roasting pan. Divide the hazelnut mixture into quarters and pat firmly over the top of each fillet, pressing down to compress the mixture and help it to adhere.

Bake until the topping is golden brown and crisp, about 10 minutes. Trim off the heads and tails of the trout, and cut the fish down the center to separate them into 4 individual fillets. Serve on warm plates, with a large spoonful of relish on the side.

519 calories, 4 grams net carbs (7 grams less 3 grams fiber), 30 grams fat (6 grams saturated)

Poultry, Game, and Meat

Whichever low-carb diet you choose to follow, none of them constitutes a license to gorge on protein. Moderation is the key—saturated fat is still bad for the heart and should be limited.

Poultry and Game

Poultry and game tend to be a little more filling than fish and shellfish, yet they are still relatively low in that old bugaboo, saturated fat. I wouldn't dream of tearing into a crisp and golden roast chicken without the skin, proving that there are certain lengths to which I will not go in the quest for health and beauty. When I was little, my dad would carve the turkey at Thanksgiving while I waited, barely able to contain myself, for the moment when he announced "Okay, the skin people can come in now." I was an only child, so that meant I was the only skin person, but he was kind enough not to call too much attention to my obsession. Left alone with a freshly roasted chicken or turkey, I can't guarantee the survival of even a shred of skin after, say, five or ten minutes (luckily, this doesn't happen often).

Now that we've dealt with the skin issue, let us celebrate the impressive ability of poultry to assume other flavors. Seasoning with salt and pepper is a start—and an absolute must—but the spice and herb repertoires really come into their own when applied judiciously to poultry. Sage and tarragon are the most bird-friendly herbs, while chiles, saffron, and curry fairly burst from the spice drawer in anticipation. Something of a floozy, poultry will go out and celebrate with anyone who comes along, whether it's citrus, as in Seared Duck Breast with Blood Orange–Veal Stock Reduction (page 108), cured pork (see both Pan-Fried Chicken Breasts with Sage and Ham Butter, page 109, and Porcini-Stuffed Turkey Thigh, page 112), or vinegar, as in the French classic *poulet sauté au vinaigre* or my Grilled Quail in Escabèche (Tomato-Vinegar) Sauce (page 118). I am always happy to come along for the party.

Meat

A number of media reports have called Atkins the "steak and bacon" diet. This statement is misleading, and false. It's true that the Atkins diet advocates more meat than the more well-rounded South Beach diet, but whichever low-carb diet you choose to follow, none of them constitutes a license to gorge on protein. Moderation is the key—saturated fat is still bad for the heart and should be limited. Other kinds of fat (especially monounsaturated fat, found in olive oil) are, strangely, turning out to be good for you (in moderation, of course). Luckily, all fats are very filling and satisfying, so you aren't likely to eat very much. In fact, I am a living example of the fact that a little fat won't make you fat (I've had a love affair with fat all my life).

Short ribs embody the succulence I love, and the Braised, Grilled, Wine-Dark Short Ribs (page 121) are one of the best examples of the genre, with the gremolata adding the necessary acidity to cut and complement the fat. On the lighter side—because fatty meats are, even for me, good only every once in awhile—there is the bright and vinegar-tart Carpaccio-Wrapped Butter Lettuce and Palm Hearts with Chimichurri Sauce (page 124) and my ode to an English spring: the pretty, bright green Seared Lamb Noisettes with Pea, Feta, and Mint Salad (page 117).

My father always said, "Moderation in all things, except moderation." I followed his lead with abandon until looking in the mirror began to scare me, yet sometimes I still skimp on moderation. In the case of meat, waiting a few weeks for a truly superb dish just makes it taste that much more wonderful.

Seared Duck Breast *with* Blood Orange–Veal Stock Reduction

SERVES 4 ∗ The fennel and blood oranges in this dish establish it firmly in the realm of wintertime food. Duck breasts can vary greatly in size; adjust the cooking time as necessary to achieve a blushing pink center. The cooking time in the recipe applies to larger breasts, 10 to 12 ounces each. Smaller breasts, 7 ounces or so, will be happier with a total cooking time of 8 to 9 minutes.

2 cups blood orange or tangerine juice (from about 7 oranges)

1 large shallot, finely chopped

1 vanilla bean

²/₃ cup veal demi-glace (see Note)

4 small or 2 large skin-on duck breasts, patted dry, and seasoned generously with salt and pepper

Fine sea salt and freshly ground black pepper

2 teaspoons canola oil

1 tablespoon cold unsalted butter

¹/₄ teaspoon balsamic vinegar

In a saucepan, combine the blood orange juice with the shallot and vanilla bean and bring to a brisk simmer. Reduce the juice by three quarters, until about ¹/₂ cup of thickened, almost jammy liquid remains, 30 to 40 minutes. Add the veal demi-glace, bring to a simmer, and reduce by about one third, to about ²/₃ cup, about 10 minutes more. The bubbles will break slowly and the liquid will be very thick. Cover the pan and set aside until serving time.

Score the fat shallowly in a wide, crisscross pattern. Place a very large sauté pan or skillet over high heat and add the canola oil (or use 2 pans to avoid overcrowding; add 1¹/₂ teaspoons oil to each pan). Turn on the range hood fan, if you have one. When the pan is very hot (after about 3 minutes), add the duck breasts, skin side down, and sear without disturbing for 3 minutes. Reduce the heat to medium and cook for 7 minutes more. Halfway through the cooking time, tilt the pan and spoon off the rendered fat. Turn the duck breasts over and cook for 3 minutes more, then transfer to a platter to rest for 3 minutes. Warm the sauce to the steaming point, then remove from the heat, remove the vanilla bean, and whisk in the butter, ¹/₄ teaspoon salt, a few turns of the peppermill, and the vinegar. Whisk until smooth.

Slice each breast crosswise about ¹/₂ inch thick and place on a warm dinner plate. Drizzle the duck generously with the sauce, and serve at once.

NOTE: Veal and poultry demi-glace are available fresh or in the freezer section of many better supermarkets, and at www.vatelcuisine.com. Do not substitute one of the nonperishable products.

314 calories, 13¹/₂ grams net carbs (14 grams less ¹/₂ gram fiber), 13 grams fat (4 grams saturated)

Pan-Fried Chicken Breasts *with* Sage *and* Ham Butter

SERVES 4 ∗ Compound butters can range from citrusy to herbal to spicy to wine-rich and, of course, garlicky. Easy to make and versatile, they can be whisked into a sauce to thicken and flavor it, or softened and served on top of grilled, roasted, or steamed meat, poultry, fish, or vegetables. I suggest making double the amount of this full-bodied, savory butter and then freezing half; it is convenient and gratifying for those nights when a seared piece of protein is all you can bring yourself to prepare.

SAGE AND HAM BUTTER

1 cup dry white wine

1 small shallot, minced

3/4 cup (6 ounces) unsalted butter, at room temperature, cut into 6 pieces

2 teaspoons fresh lemon juice

2 tablespoons minced ham

1 tablespoon finely chopped fresh sage

1/4 teaspoon fine sea salt

Freshly ground black pepper

4 boneless, skinless chicken breasts, preferably free-range or kosher, patted dry

Fine sea salt and freshly ground black pepper

2 teaspoons unsalted butter

2 teaspoons canola or olive oil

3/4 cup dry white wine

3 tablespoons water

To prepare the butter, in a small saucepan, combine the wine and shallot and place over low heat. Simmer, uncovered, for 12 to 15 minutes, until the liquid is reduced to about 2 tablespoons. Cool for 10 minutes. In a mixing bowl, combine the butter, lemon juice, ham, and sage and stir to combine. Whisk in the reduced wine and shallot mixture and add the salt and some pepper. The butter should be creamy; if it is refrigerated before serving (up to 1 week is fine), return to room temperature before serving.

Place 4 dinner plates and a baking dish in a low oven to warm. Pound the chicken breasts just slightly to an even thickness of slightly over 1/4 inch. Season both sides generously with salt and pepper.

Place a very large skillet over high heat and add the butter and oil (or use 2 skillets and make the sauce in one of the pans; on no account should the chicken be crowded). When the butter has melted and the foam has subsided, add the chicken breasts without allowing them to touch one another, and cook for 2 minutes without disturbing. Turn and cook for 2 to 2 1/2 minutes more, until firm and done through to the center with no pink remaining. Transfer the chicken breasts to the baking dish in the oven, and turn off the oven. Immediately add the wine and water to the pan. Still over high heat, stir the bubbling mixture with a wooden spoon, stirring and scraping the pan to release all the flavorful bits. When about 2 tablespoons of liquid remain, remove it from the heat and let stand for 1 1/2 minutes to cool just slightly. Add the sage and ham butter and immediately whisk until the butter has emulsified into the sauce, thickening it slightly. Place a chicken breast on each warm plate, top with several generous spoonfuls of the sauce, and serve.

581 calories, 7 grams net carbs (7 grams less 0 grams fiber), 46 grams fat (25 grams saturated)

Wine-Braised Chicken Thighs with Green Olives and Herbs

SERVES 4 ＊ The herbs and wine here provide needed acidity, without which the dish would be too heavy and cloying; the pancetta adds that tiny accent of cured-pork flavor that always marries so blissfully with poultry, game, and fish. Italians have recognized this affinity for generations—witness *saltimbocca alla Romana*. It provides an earthy complexity that chicken alone—especially in these days of supermarket chicken—simply cannot aspire to. This dish is chunky, rustic, voluptuously full of flavor, and, to me, sublime.

8 bone-in, skinless chicken thighs

Extra virgin olive oil, for brushing

Fine sea salt and freshly ground black pepper

2 ounces pancetta, finely chopped

1 onion, coarsely chopped

Large branch fresh rosemary

Large sprig fresh thyme

5 cloves garlic, minced or pressed

1 1/4 cups dry white wine

1 1/2 cups chicken broth, preferably homemade

1 slice lemon, about 1/4 inch thick

1 cup pitted, halved picholine, lucques, or other brine-cured green olives

Preheat the oven to 400°F. Brush the chicken thighs on all sides with olive oil, then season generously with salt and pepper. Place in a large, heavy, flameproof roasting pan and roast for 20 minutes, until golden. Reduce the oven to 325°F.

Transfer the chicken to a platter and pour almost all the fat from the pan. Place the pan over medium heat and add the pancetta, onion, rosemary, and thyme. Sauté for about 5 minutes, until the onion is tender, then add the garlic and stir for 1 minute. Return the chicken to the pan and add the wine. Bring to a simmer and reduce by about half, 8 to 10 minutes, tipping the pan and skimming the fat occasionally. Add the chicken broth, lemon slice, 1/4 teaspoon salt, and a generous grinding of pepper. Bring to a boil, cover tightly with foil, and transfer to the oven. Cook for 30 minutes, turn the chicken pieces over, add the olives, and continue cooking for about 20 minutes more, until the chicken is very tender. Transfer the chicken to a warm platter, cover with foil, and reduce the sauce over high heat to concentrate the juices, stirring, for 4 to 5 minutes. Remove the vestiges of the herb branches and the lemon slice, return the chicken to the pan for a moment, and serve, spooning plenty of the chunky sauce over the top.

549 calories, 4 grams net carbs (5 grams less 1 gram fiber), 37 grams fat (10 grams saturated)

Porcini-Stuffed Turkey Thigh

SERVES 6 * After fighting a twelve-year losing battle trying to get my English friends excited about Thanksgiving when I lived in England, I am now a giddy aficionado of this traditional holiday. Every year I'm reminded how delicious turkey can be (as long as it's brined) and wonder why we Americans don't serve it more often. So in search of a smaller-sized—yet still festive and tasty—portion, and loving dark meat as I do, the decision was easy. Sure, turkey breast is light and convenient, but where's the succulence and flavor? In this dish, the prosciutto is not intended as a component; it's a patch that holds in the stuffing, incidentally providing a little savor. The cured-pork element is, instead, found in the chunky, aromatic, and wine-dark confit. The stuffing and the confit both also work exceedingly well with boneless pork loin.

1 turkey thigh, about 2¹/₂ pounds (see Note)

1 apple, peeled, cored, and coarsely chopped

1 small onion, coarsely chopped

8 cups water

¹/₃ cup coarse sea salt or kosher salt

5 black peppercorns

1 cinnamon stick

1 pod star anise

1 bay leaf

ONION-PANCETTA CONFIT (OPTIONAL)

2 ounces pancetta, finely chopped

1 tablespoon good olive oil

2 large red onions, sliced about ³/₈ inch thick

2 sprigs fresh thyme

³/₄ cup dry red wine, such as cabernet sauvignon

¹/₄ cup balsamic vinegar

¹/₄ teaspoon fine sea salt

Freshly ground black pepper

From the back, cut down the length of the turkey thigh bone, then cut around the bone carefully and remove it. In a large glass or plastic container, combine the apple, onion, water, salt, peppercorns, cinnamon, star anise, and bay leaf. Stir with a wooden spoon until the salt dissolves, then immerse the thigh, making sure it is covered with water. Refrigerate for 6 hours.

To prepare the onion-pancetta confit, place a large skillet or sauté pan over medium-low heat and add the pancetta and olive oil. Cook, stirring, until the pancetta has begun to render out a little fat, about 3 minutes. Add the onions and thyme and cook, stirring occasionally, for about 20 minutes, until softened and slightly caramelized. Add the wine and vinegar and cook until most of the liquid has been absorbed, about 20 minutes more. Remove the remains of the thyme sprigs, stir in the salt and a generous grinding of black pepper, and remove from the heat. Let stand at room temperature for up to 2 hours before serving, or cover and refrigerate for up to 5 days. Be sure to return the confit to room temperature before serving, to awaken the flavors.

To prepare the stuffing, cover the porcini with very hot water and let stand for 20 minutes to rehydrate. Squeeze very firmly to extract the water, and chop finely. In a mixing bowl, combine the porcini with the spinach, pine nuts, and goat cheese. Add the salt, a generous grinding of black pepper, the nutmeg, and egg and combine thoroughly.

PORCINI STUFFING

$^1/_2$ ounce dried porcini mushrooms

1 (10 ounce) package chopped frozen spinach, completely thawed and squeezed firmly to remove excess water

2 tablespoons pine nuts, toasted in a dry skillet until aromatic (about 3 minutes)

2 ounces fresh goat cheese, at room temperature

$^1/_4$ teaspoon fine sea salt

Freshly ground black pepper

$^1/_4$ teaspoon ground nutmeg

1 large egg, lightly beaten

2 slices prosciutto, $^1/_8$ inch thick (thicker than prosciutto is normally cut; ask your deli counter)

2 tablespoons unsalted butter, at room temperature

Preheat the oven to 400°F.

Remove the turkey from the brine and pat dry thoroughly with paper towels, then open it out like a book and place it on a cutting board, skin side down. With a long, narrow knife, butterfly the thickest parts of the thigh on either side (make a long, horizontal slice down to about $^3/_4$ inch from the other side) to make more room for the stuffing. Firmly pack the stuffing down the center and sides to within 1 inch of the ends. Close up the book, enclosing the stuffing, and place the prosciutto over the top to hold the stuffing in. Tie the meat firmly in 3 or 4 places with fine kitchen twine. Place the thigh prosciutto–side up on a rack in a roasting pan, rub all over with the butter, and season all sides generously with pepper only.

Roast for 20 minutes, then reduce the heat to 325°F, turn skin side up, and roast for 25 to 30 minutes more, until an instant-read thermometer inserted in the middle of the thickest part of the meat (not the stuffing) reads 170°F.

Remove from the oven and let stand, loosely covered with foil, for 10 minutes. If desired, discard the prosciutto. Carve about $^3/_4$ inch thick and serve on warmed plates, with a generous spoonful of the onion-pancetta confit on the side, if desired.

NOTE: The size of turkey thighs available in the supermarket varies greatly depending on the time of year. If the thighs are smaller, cook 2 at once and divide the stuffing between them. Calculate the cooking time based on the prestuffing weight of the larger thigh— not the combined weight of 2 or 3 thighs—and allow about 20 minutes per pound plus 5 to 10 minutes extra.

Turkey, stuffing, and confit: 515 calories, 9 grams net carbs (11 grams less 2 grams fiber), 27 grams fat (9 grams saturated)

Turkey and stuffing only: 434 calories, 3 grams net carbs (5 grams less 2 grams fiber), 23 grams fat (9 grams saturated)

Rabbit *with* Saffron *and* Fennel Ragoût *and* Whole-Wheat Linguine

SERVES 4 * Five minutes inland from my home on the expatriate-packed Costa del Sol, one suddenly entered the real Spain. A tiny "restaurant" on the road into Casares consistently served a rustic, peasant-style version of this refined dish, using the faux saffron called *colorante,* and sherry in place of the Pernod. It's nice to have something to mop up this creamy, flavorful sauce, and whole-wheat linguine—in the small portions used here—makes a fine candidate. Just be sure your daily carbohydrate count is low on the evening you plan to serve the dish.

2 tablespoons white wine vinegar

1/2 teaspoon loosely packed saffron threads

1 rabbit, 2 1/2 to 3 pounds, cut into 6 to 8 serving pieces, rinsed well and patted dry

Fine sea salt and white pepper, preferably freshly ground

All-purpose flour, for dusting

3 tablespoons extra virgin olive oil

1/4 cup Pernod or anisette

Half a small onion, finely chopped

1 small bulb fennel, trimmed, quartered, cored, and slivered crosswise

4 cloves garlic, thinly sliced

2 1/4 cups dry white wine

1/2 teaspoon ground fennel seeds (see Note)

1/3 cup crème fraîche

2 ounces dried whole-wheat linguine or fettuccine

1 tablespoon finely snipped chives, for serving

Preheat the oven to 375°F. In a small saucer, combine the vinegar and saffron and let the saffron soak while you sear the rabbit.

Be sure the rabbit pieces are completely dry, then season on both sides with salt and white pepper. Dust the pieces very lightly with flour (preferably from a shaker), and shake to remove the excess.

Place a large, oven-safe sauté pan over medium-high heat and add the oil. When it is very hot, add the rabbit pieces and sear them without disturbing for 5 minutes. Turn over and sear for 5 minutes more, until golden brown. Pull the pan off the heat for a moment and add the Pernod. Return to the heat (you can flame the Pernod if desired, but the alcohol will burn off by itself). Sizzle for 30 seconds, then transfer the rabbit to a platter and set it aside.

Reduce the heat to medium-low and add the onion, fennel, and garlic to the pan. Cook, stirring, for about 7 minutes, until the onion is softened but not at all browned. Add the wine vinegar–saffron mixture, and ground fennel, and return the rabbit to the pan. Bring the liquid to a simmer on top of the stove, then cover the pan tightly with foil, place the lid on top securely, and braise in the oven for about 1 1/4 hours, turning the rabbit over halfway through, until tender.

Bring a large saucepan of salted water to a boil for cooking the pasta.

continued

Transfer the pan back to the stovetop and, with tongs, carefully transfer the rabbit pieces to a serving platter. Cover the rabbit with foil and keep warm in the turned-off oven while you finish the sauce. Add the crème fraîche, $^1/_4$ teaspoon salt, and a good pinch of pepper to the pan and bring to a rapid simmer over medium-high heat. Cook until the chunky sauce has thickened nicely, stirring or whisking frequently. This will take from 5 to 15 minutes, depending on how juicy the rabbit was.

While the sauce is reducing, warm 4 plates in the turned-off oven and cook the pasta until al dente. Drain thoroughly and mound a little nest of pasta on each warm plate. Top with a piece or two of rabbit and spoon a generous amount of sauce over the top. Scatter with a few chives and serve immediately.

NOTE: Ground fennel is available from good spice merchants, or you can grind fennel seeds in a mortar and pestle or a coffee grinder reserved for grinding spices.

891 calories, 15 grams net carbs (18 grams less 3 grams fiber), 34 grams fat (10 grams saturated)

Seared Lamb Noisettes *with* Pea, Feta, *and* Mint Salad

SERVES 4 ∗ This dish is an English-Mediterranean hybrid that is all about spring: spring lamb, fresh garden peas, and bright, clean mint. Noisettes of lamb—very popular in England but rarely seen in the United States—are made from racks of lamb. Ask the butcher to carefully cut the meat from the rack in one piece, leaving some of the fat intact, and then tie it to maintain the round shape. An 8-rib rack will yield 8 noisettes and should be tied in 8 places equidistant from one another before being cut crosswise. For large appetites you may want to double the quantity of lamb (this will not affect the carbohydrate count but will increase the calorie and fat counts by about 30 percent).

Minced or grated zest of 1 scrubbed lemon

$1/3$ cup fresh lemon juice (from about 2 lemons)

2 large cloves garlic, minced or pressed

$2^{1}/_{2}$ tablespoons extra virgin olive oil

8 noisettes of lamb, 1 to $1^{1}/_{4}$ inches thick, trimmed and tied (about 1 pound)

2 cups shelled fresh peas (or use thawed frozen petits pois)

Fine sea salt and freshly ground black pepper

2 tablespoons finely chopped fresh mint

Pinch of ground allspice

1 teaspoon unsalted butter

1 tablespoon water

3 ounces mild French feta cheese, cut into $1/4$-inch cubes

In a shallow glass or ceramic dish, whisk the lemon zest and juice, garlic, and 1 tablespoon of the olive oil. Add the lamb and turn once, then cover with plastic wrap and let stand for 15 minutes. Turn over again and let stand for 15 minutes more.

Prepare an ice bath, then blanch the fresh peas for 1 to 2 minutes in lightly salted boiling water, until not quite tender. Immediately drain and then plunge into the ice bath. Drain well and spread on a layer of paper towels. (If using thawed frozen petits pois, simply roll them around gently on paper towels to dry.)

In a bowl, combine the peas, $1/2$ tablespoon of the olive oil, salt, pepper, and mint. Toss together gently and spread into a thin, even layer on a flat serving platter. Pat the noisettes dry with paper towels (reserve the marinade) and season both sides generously with salt, pepper, and a tiny pinch of allspice.

Place a large, heavy sauté pan or skillet over high heat and add the remaining tablespoon of olive oil and the butter (use 2 pans if necessary to avoid crowding). When the butter is starting to brown, add and sear the noisettes for 2 minutes. Turn over with tongs, reduce the heat to medium-low and cook for about 2 minutes more, for medium-rare. Transfer the noisettes to the platter, placing them on top of the peas. Add the remaining marinade and 1 tablespoon of water to the pan and deglaze over high heat for a minute, until the liquid is reduced to about 2 tablespoons. Drizzle the juices over the lamb and the peas, scatter the feta around the lamb, and serve.

421 calories, 10 grams net carbs (14 grams less 4 grams fiber), 23 grams fat (8 grams saturated)

Grilled Quail *in* Escabèche (Tomato-Vinegar) Sauce

SERVES 4 ∗ In the extended family of Latin and Latin American cuisines, escabèche is a relative of ceviche. Both depend on acidity for their character: in ceviche, fish or shellfish is "cooked" by generous quantities of lemon or lime juice, while in escabèche the meat is first cooked and then marinated in a vinegar-tomato mixture. Quail can be fiddly to eat but are worth pursuing because of the gentle yet slightly gamy, rich flavor; butterflying makes eating them easier, but best of all is to grill completely boneless quail. Boning quail is a laborious business, and unless you can find them already boned, a simpler solution is to remove just the thigh bones and part of the rib cage. Be sure to use your sharpest, smallest knife so you get all the meat off the bones. For hungry diners, serve 3 quail per person. This will not affect the carbohydrate count.

ESCABÈCHE SAUCE

2 teaspoons olive or canola oil

4 cloves garlic, minced or pressed

$1^1/_2$ teaspoons ground coriander

2 tablespoons sherry vinegar

1 tablespoon red wine vinegar

2 teaspoons tomato paste

$1^1/_2$ cups tomato juice

2 sprigs fresh cilantro

2 sprigs fresh thyme

1 bay leaf

$^1/_4$ cup finely diced red onion

$^1/_4$ cup finely diced red bell pepper

$^1/_4$ cup finely diced yellow bell pepper

2 tablespoons drained capers

$^1/_8$ teaspoon fine sea salt

Pinch of freshly ground black pepper

2 dashes Tabasco sauce

To prepare the sauce, place a large, nonstick skillet over medium-low heat and add the olive oil. Sauté the garlic and the coriander together, stirring, for $1^1/_2$ minutes. Don't allow the garlic to brown. Add the sherry and vinegar and stir to deglaze the pan. Simmer for about a minute to reduce slightly, then stir in the tomato paste and tomato juice. Add the cilantro, thyme, and bay leaf and bring to a boil, then reduce the heat so the sauce barely simmers. Cook, partially covered, over very low heat for about 20 minutes, until slightly thickened. Remove the herb stems and bay leaf, and stir in the red onion, red and yellow pepper, capers, salt, pepper, and Tabasco. Cover and set aside at the back of the stove until serving time (or, for a summer lunch, let cool to room temperature).

Rinse the quail and pat dry thoroughly, inside and out, with paper towels. With kitchen shears, cut out the backbones and press down on the breastbones with the palm of your hand to flatten them. If desired, remove the thigh bones and part of the breast cage, scraping so you don't remove too much meat (this will make them easier to eat.) Season both sides generously with salt, pepper, and oregano. Sprinkle with a little olive oil and rub into the flesh of both sides. Wrap each quail with a few strips of pancetta and skewer with toothpicks in several places around the edges, to secure the pancetta.

continued

8 quail, 3 to 4 ounces each

Fine sea salt and freshly ground black pepper

$^1/_2$ teaspoon dried oregano, crumbled

1 tablespoon good olive oil

4 ounces thinly sliced pancetta, unraveled into long, curly strips

1 tablespoon finely chopped fresh cilantro, for serving

Preheat a charcoal or gas grill for medium-heat grilling, and oil the grate. Grill the quail, turning once or twice, until firm and golden but still a little pink at the bone, 3 to 5 minutes. Do not overcook, or they will be tough. Transfer to the pan of sauce and, if desired, discard the pancetta. Let stand for 5 to 15 minutes, spooning the sauce over the tops. Serve with plenty of sauce and a pinch of cilantro.

550 calories, 9 grams net carbs (10 grams less 1 gram fiber), 36 grams fat (9 grams saturated)

Braised, Grilled, Wine-Dark Short Ribs

SERVES 4 ∗ At first glance, the method here may seem complex, but the result is nothing even a rib aficionado is likely to have come across before. The inside is succulent, collagen-rich meat, the outside crusty and crisp, almost as if the ribs have been deep-fried. Wow.

Note the high calorie count on these rich and meaty ribs. It's an example of how low carb doesn't always mean low-calorie. You can't completely ignore the fat content, even if some diets do advocate high-fat dining. Short ribs are so luscious because they have a lot of intramuscular fat that can't be trimmed off and doesn't all cook away. So be aware and serve these ribs with a salad and a green vegetable. And be sure to skip the cheese course at this dinner.

You'll need to allow about 6½ hours for cooking the short ribs, plus 24 hours' marinating time.

12 cloves garlic, lightly crushed

1½ teaspoons coarse sea salt

Freshly ground black pepper

2½ to 3 pounds bone-in short ribs

2 tablespoons good olive oil

¼ cup coarsely chopped carrot

¼ cup coarsely chopped onion

¼ cup coarsely chopped leek, white and light green parts

2 sprigs fresh thyme

1 bay leaf

2½ cups dry red wine, such as cabernet sauvignon

3 tablespoons red wine vinegar

1 cup veal, beef, or rich chicken broth

Fine sea salt and freshly ground black pepper

Place 4 cloves of the garlic and 1½ teaspoons coarse sea salt in a mortar, and pulverize to a paste with a pestle (or mince and smash with a large, heavy chef's knife). Rub all sides of the ribs with this paste, and grind some pepper over all sides. Let stand at room temperature for 1 hour.

Place a large, heavy saucepan over low heat and add 1 tablespoon of the oil. Add the carrot, onion, leek, and remaining 8 cloves garlic. Sauté, stirring, for 5 to 6 minutes, until softened but not browned, then stir in the thyme, bay leaf, wine, and vinegar. Bring to a simmer, then remove from the heat and transfer to a large, heatproof bowl or measuring cup, to help it cool faster. Cool to room temperature.

Place the ribs and wine mixture in a large, heavy-duty resealable plastic bag. Seal well, and refrigerate for at least 8 but preferably 24 hours, turning once or twice.

Preheat the oven to 275°F. Remove the ribs from the marinade and scrape off all the vegetables. Pour the marinade (with all the vegetables) into a saucepan, add the broth, and bring to a simmer. Remove from the heat.

continued

LIME GREMOLATA

Minced or grated zest of 2 limes

1 teaspoon finely chopped flat-leaf parsley

1 teaspoon minced or pressed garlic

1 tablespoon unsalted butter, at room temperature, cut into 4 pieces

Pat the ribs dry thoroughly with paper towels and season generously on all four sides with fine sea salt and pepper. Place a very large, heavy skillet or sauté pan over medium-high heat and add the remaining tablespoon of oil. When it is very hot, add the ribs and brown for about 2¹/₂ minutes on each of the four sides (or sauté in batches to avoid overcrowding). Transfer the ribs to a small roasting pan and pour the warm marinade over them. Cover the pan tightly with foil and roast for 3 to 3¹/₂ hours, turning the ribs over halfway through, until fork-tender but not completely falling apart. Remove from the oven, uncover, and let stand for 5 minutes.

With tongs, transfer the ribs to a platter and remove the bones. Trim away any obvious gristle and surface fat, without cutting the ribs into very small pieces. (If desired, the beef can now be refrigerated for up to 2 days before the final grilling.)

Strain the cooking liquid, discarding the vegetables, and skim off the fat. (Use a fat separator or, if the ribs won't be grilled immediately, refrigerate the liquid until the fat solidifies.) In a saucepan over high heat, simmer the liquid rapidly for 10 to 20 minutes, until reduced to just under 1 cup of very dark liquid. Remove from the heat, taste for seasoning, then cover and keep warm while you grill the ribs.

To prepare the gremolata, in a small bowl, combine and toss together the lime zest, parsley, and garlic.

Preheat a charcoal or gas grill, cast-iron grill pan, or broiler until very hot. Sear the chunks of meat for 1 to 2 minutes on all sides until heated through, crisp, and browned. Whisk the butter into the sauce, to give it a glossy sheen.

Serve on warm plates, drizzling with plenty of the sauce and scattering 2 generous pinches of lime gremolata over each serving.

815 calories, 8 grams net carbs (9 grams less 1 gram fiber), 46 grams fat (18 grams saturated)

Carpaccio-Wrapped Butter Lettuce *and* Palm Hearts *with* Chimichurri Sauce

SERVES 4 * Carpaccio has always been on my menu, though it is difficult to make at home unless you happen to own an electric meat-slicer. To make the meat as firm as possible before slicing, freeze it for about 30 minutes (see the beef tataki on page 14). Better yet, call your butcher ahead of time and ask him to freeze and then slice the meat (savvy butchers are used to carpaccio calls). My latest solution is to buy meat that is sliced for sukiyaki from a Japanese supermarket. It's already cut paper-thin, and there's no waste! This dish is an Argentinean take on carpaccio, and it has all the same benefits: cool, clean, beefy flavor, spicy sauce, and texture.

$^2/_3$ cup seasoned rice vinegar

1 tablespoon soy sauce

1 tablespoon Thai or Vietnamese fish sauce

1 tablespoon fresh lime juice

1 teaspoon toasted sesame oil

$^1/_2$ teaspoon dried red pepper flakes

$^1/_2$ teaspoon coarsely ground black pepper

$^1/_4$ teaspoon fine sea salt

CHIMICHURRI SAUCE

1 cup firmly packed flat-leaf parsley, leaves and tender stems only (about 2 ounces)

4 cloves garlic, quartered

$1^1/_2$ tablespoons fresh oregano leaves

$^1/_3$ cup extra virgin olive oil

$1^1/_2$ teaspoons coarse sea salt

$^1/_2$ teaspoon freshly ground pepper

$^1/_8$ teaspoon dried red pepper flakes (optional)

2 tablespoons white wine vinegar

In a small saucepan, combine the vinegar, soy sauce, fish sauce, lime juice, sesame oil, pepper flakes, pepper, and salt. Bring to just below the simmering point and immediately remove from the heat. Pour into a wide shallow bowl or baking dish and cool to room temperature.

To prepare the chimichurri sauce, in a food processor or by hand, combine and finely chop the parsley, garlic, and oregano. Transfer the mixture to a small bowl and stir in the olive oil, salt, pepper, and pepper flakes. Use at once or cover and refrigerate for up to 4 hours. Just before serving, stir in the vinegar (adding it too soon will turn the parsley gray).

Fifteen minutes before serving, add the sliced beef to the marinade, tossing gently to coat evenly; cover and refrigerate.

12 slices (about 12 ounces) thinly sliced lean boneless sirloin or rib eye (available at Japanese supermarkets, or ask the butcher to freeze and slice the beef for you; slices should be less than $1/8$ inch thick)

4 pieces (about 3 ounces) hearts of palm, julienned lengthwise

1 small leek, white part only, halved, well washed, and cut into lengthwise julienne

1 small head butter lettuce, pale inner heart only, leaves separated and julienned

Fine sea salt and freshly ground black pepper

In a medium bowl, toss the palm hearts, leek, and lettuce julienne together to mix evenly. Season with salt and pepper. Working with one slice of beef at a time, place a slice on the work surface and top with a generous pinch of the leek mixture (stack the julienne lengthwise, like a bunch of twigs; they will stick out at the ends). Loosely roll up the beef to enclose the crisp ingredients, and place on a serving platter. Repeat with the remaining slices. Drizzle a little chimichurri sauce over each roll and serve at once, allowing 3 rolls per person.

291 calories, 11 grams net carbs (12 grams less 1 gram fiber), 15 grams fat (3 grams saturated)

Smoked Bacon *and* Pork Tenderloin Skewers *with* Three-Citrus Mojo

SERVES 4 ∗ I have served some variation of this dish at least once a month since I lived in England, when I found a version containing bread cubes in the superb and very collectible series Time-Life: *The Good Cook*. (The dish has become Cuban in style this year, but it's all part of the journey.) The bacon bastes and flavors the pork cubes, and the dish ends up as a sort of grilled salad when you push the cubes off the skewer onto the lettuce and toss it all together with the spicy, citrusy mojo (a mojo is a Cuban sauce). It's perfect fodder for a poolside party, with or without children. Add a classic daiquiri on the rocks (use Splenda in place of the sugar) topped with a floater of 12-year-old Cuban rum. Heaven.

THREE-CITRUS MOJO

Minced or grated zest of half a scrubbed orange

Minced or grated zest of half a scrubbed lime

Minced or grated zest of half a scrubbed lemon

2 tablespoons fresh orange juice

2 teaspoons fresh lime juice

1 teaspoon fresh lemon juice

3 tablespoons finely diced red onion

3 cloves garlic, minced or pressed

Fine sea salt and freshly ground black pepper

2 tablespoons finely chopped flat-leaf parsley

3 tablespoons extra virgin olive oil

1¼ pounds pork fillet, cut into 1-inch cubes (about 20 cubes)

20 pieces, ¾ inch square, unsmoked bacon (about 4 slices)

2 tablespoons good olive oil

½ teaspoon ground cumin

Half a small head of iceberg lettuce, thinly sliced and fluffed

To prepare the mojo, in a glass or ceramic bowl, combine and stir together the orange, lime, and lemon zest and juice, onion, garlic, ½ teaspoon of salt, a little pepper, parsley, and olive oil. If desired, cover and refrigerate for up to 12 hours. Return to room temperature before serving.

In a mixing bowl, combine the pork, bacon, olive oil, ¾ teaspoon of salt, a few turns of the peppermill, and the cumin. Toss together and let stand at room temperature for 15 minutes.

Prepare a charcoal or gas grill for medium-heat grilling, or heat an indoor broiler or well-seasoned cast-iron grill pan to high heat.

Thread pork and bacon alternately onto 4 long bamboo skewers or 8 shorter skewers. Wrap the blunt end of each skewer with foil to keep it from catching fire. Grill the skewers for 3 to 4 minutes on each of the 4 sides, until the pork is firm and just slightly golden. Spread a rectangle of lettuce on each of 4 plates and top with a skewer (or 2 if short), removing the foil. Spoon about 2½ tablespoons of the chunky mojo over the top of each one, and serve at once.

388 calories, 3 grams net carbs (4 grams less 1 gram fiber), 26 grams fat (5 grams saturated)

The Cheese Course

Cheese should be enjoyed in moderation on a low-carb regime, but luckily it is so satisfying that a little goes a long way.

CHOOSING FROM THE CHEESE CART has always been one of my favorite parts of dining out in Europe, and now the cheese cart has come to America. In New York there is a restaurant called Artisanal that specializes in cheese and features one hundred out of a possible two hundred different kinds on any given day. One of the most popular restaurants in Los Angeles, A.O.C., has a cheese bar, and it's always packed. At The Inn at Little Washington in Virginia, the cheese cart has a cow's head and tail, and moos disarmingly as it approaches the table. Cheese should be enjoyed in moderation on a low-carb regime, but luckily it is so satisfying that a little goes a long way. A nibble of cheese will go much further in sating the appetite than the equivalent weight of bread or breadsticks, and at around 1 carb per ounce sits far better on the waistline than 1 ounce of breadsticks (about 2 bread-sticks), at a whopping 21 carbs. This is especially true if you select interesting, unique, and culturally diverse cheeses and pair them with care. If you have traveled to the country of origin of your selections, treat the cheese course as a trip down memory lane; if not, let it be the appetizer for future travel plans. I do feel, however, that passing an unwieldy cheese platter is passé; the cheese soon begins to look hacked up, and there is a lot of awkward reaching after the first pass. Instead, I prefer to place two carefully chosen cheeses on individual serving plates and accompany them with the perfect, culturally appropriate beverage and a complementary nibble.

NOTE: In every case (except for soft and exceedingly fresh, perishable cheeses like burrata), please allow your carefully selected—and often quite expensive—cheese to stand at room temperature, under a cheese cloche if desired, for at least 2 and up to 24 hours before serving. Chilled cheese is tasteless!

Cabrales and Manchego with Celery Hearts and Pedro Jimenez

SERVES 4 * Cabrales is a rich and intense aged, blue-veined goat's milk cheese from the Asturias region of Spain. Almost like a hick country cousin to the more refined, lily white Roquefort, Cabrales is considered by some cheese connoisseurs to be one of the greatest unsung cheeses of the world. Manchego is unarguably the pride of Spain, and is not only sung about frequently, but quite widely available. It has a distinctive crosshatch pattern on the rind, which is not edible. If sheep's milk manchego is hard to find, substitute a cow's milk version. If you buy your cheese from a reputable purveyor and plan to serve it within 24 hours, please do not refrigerate it. The flavor will be sadly diminished, like looking at a beautiful landscape through a piece of mesh fabric.

2 small, pale inner hearts of celery, with leaves, halved lengthwise

3 ounces Cabrales cheese

3 ounces aged sheep's milk manchego cheese (see Note)

4 ounces Pedro Jimenez (sweet, red Spanish wine with a slight sherry character), or port

In a bowl, cover the halved celery hearts with cold water and add a good handful of ice cubes. Let stand in the refrigerator for 1 hour, to crisp.

Bring the cheeses to room temperature for at least 1 hour, if they have been refrigerated.

Drain the celery hearts and pat dry thoroughly with paper towels. Place a half heart on each of 4 plates. Divide each of the cheeses into 4 equal chunks and place a piece of each cheese on one side of each celery heart. Pour the Pedro Jimenez into 4 tiny glasses, such as grappa or shot glasses, and place opposite the cheese. Serve at once.

NOTE: For a fantastic array of Spanish products, including white anchovies, jamón serrano, a fantastic selection of cheeses, olives, olive oils, wines (including Pedro Jimenez), and chorizo, visit the charming and friendly family-run La Espanola, at http://donajuana.com, or www.tienda.com.

158 calories, 5 grams net carbs (6 grams less 1 gram fiber),
8 grams fat (6 grams saturated)

Epoisses and Roquefort with Walnuts and Marc de Bourgogne

SERVES 4 * One of the greatest cheeses from arguably the finest eating region in France, Burgundy, Epoisses should be an unpasteurized cow's milk cheese with a soft, edible rind. Unfortunately, in this country, it is made from pasteurized milk (when, oh when, will this ridiculous law end?). Epoisses is a washed-rind cheese and, happily, the liquid used for washing it is Marc de Bourgogne, the fiery, grappa-style eau de vie made from the dregs of the wine grapes after Burgundy's great wines are made. If unavailable, substitute a Pont l'Eveque or a Livarot. Roquefort needs no introduction—but be sure to locate a ripe, soft specimen.

3 ounces Epoisses cheese

3 ounces Roquefort cheese

8 walnuts, purchased from a reputable dealer with high turnover to ensure freshness

4 ounces Marc de Bourgogne or Marc from another wine-making region

Bring the cheeses to room temperature for at least 1 hour, preferably 3. Carefully shell the walnuts and pick over the meat to remove any shells.

Cut each cheese into 4 equal portions and arrange on 4 attractive plates. Divide the walnuts among 4 soy sauce saucers, and pour the Marc into 4 pretty shot glasses or square glass sake cups. Place a saucer of nuts and a glass of Marc on each plate opposite the two cheeses, and serve.

334 calories, 3 grams net carbs (4 grams less 1 gram fiber), 23 grams fat (9 grams saturated)

Scamorza *and* Pecorino Romano *with* Dried Figs *and* Vin Santo

SERVES 4 ✳ Similar to mozzarella but with a denser, drier texture, scamorza is available either plain or smoked. Pecorino Romano is a tangy, salty sheep's milk cousin of Parmigiano-Reggiano, with a granular texture and an inedible rind. The flavors of these two powerful, assertive, and forward cheeses, when paired with the sweet figs and luscious vin santo, are enough to knock your socks into the next county. At 10 grams of net carbs each, dried figs are definitely an indulgence. But they are full of flavor and fiber, and just one makes a perfect, unmistakably Italian complement to these smoky and salty cheeses.

3 ounces smoked scamorza cheese

3 ounces Pecorino Romano cheese

4 dried figs

4 ounces vin santo

Bring the cheeses to room temperature for at least 1 hour, preferably 3. Divide each cheese into 4 equal chunks.

Snip off the fig stems and cut down almost to the base, then cut again through the center, perpendicular to the first cut, so the quarters open out like a flower. Place a fig on each of 4 small, pretty plates, and place the 2 cheeses opposite. Pour the vin santo into tiny glasses (grappa glasses work well), and place one on the side of each plate.

234 calories, 15 grams net carbs (17 grams less 2 grams fiber), 9 grams fat (6 grams saturated)

Kefalotyri Grilled in a Vine Leaf, and Feta with Kalamata Olives and Retsina

SERVES 4 * The aroma of Greece is unique, soft and perfumed with hints of pine and eucalyptus permeating the land, infusing Greek cheeses and wines alike with a palpable and savory sense of being there. Since I am a lover of sheep's milk cheeses, in this travelogue you find two: kefalotyri—a good melting cheese that is reminiscent of a Romano, though softer and less salty—and feta, the classic, much-used soft sheep's milk cheese that has been embraced worldwide. Please find a Greek feta, not a French one (far milder in flavor) for this lovely yet very assertive dish.

4 brine-packed grape leaves, base of tough central stems trimmed away

4 ounces Greek kefalotyri cheese, cut into 4 rectangles, 2 by 4 inches and 1 inch thick

1 small clove garlic, minced

Grated or minced zest of half a lemon

Freshly ground black pepper

Olive oil, for brushing

4 ounces Greek feta cheese, cut into 4 equal squares and kept chilled

12 Kalamata olives, drained

4 ounces imported retsina, well chilled

Rinse the vine leaves gently under cold running water and pat dry. Place 2 leaves on a work surface, slightly overlapping, and place 1 piece of the kefalotyri cheese in the center. Scatter one fourth of the garlic and lemon zest on the cheese, sprinkle with some pepper, and wrap up into a secure packet. Place seam side down on a platter. Repeat with the remaining leaves and kefalotyri. Refrigerate for up to 2 hours, if desired. Let return to room temperature for 15 minutes before grilling.

Preheat an outdoor charcoal or gas grill to low heat, or heat a well-seasoned, ridged cast-iron grill pan over medium-low heat. Brush the packets lightly with olive oil. Grill for about 5 minutes on each side, or until the edges of the leaves start to scorch and the whole package feels soft when gently pressed. The cheese should be just beginning to ooze from the edges.

Place a cheese package and a square of feta on each of 4 plates and scatter the olives around them (or place the olives in a sake cup). Place a shot glass of retsina on each plate and serve at once.

248 calories, 4 grams net carbs (4 grams less 0 grams fiber), 17 grams fat (9 grams saturated)

Dessert

The key to
finishing a low-carb
meal feeling satisfied
is plenty of variation
and a procession
of small but
filling courses.

IF YOU CRAVE SOMETHING SWEET after dinner, these refined confections will fill that need. The key to finishing a low-carb meal feeling satisfied is plenty of variation and a procession of small but filling courses. There are plenty of low-carb cookbooks out there that will tell you how to make fake cake, faux cookies, and pretend pie, but this is not one of them. I prefer to eat food in the way it tastes best, as it was intended to be. If I really need to have a cookie (and everyone does from time to time), I'll have a real one and keep myself strictly to plan for the next couple of days.

Although, I normally am categorically against anything faux, I honestly do find Splenda to be a wonderful product, when used in moderation. Its sweetening effect, which seems free of aftertaste or bitterness, has been a wonderful solution for my morning tea. (After all those years in England, I wasn't about to start having my eye-opening cuppa unsweetened when I started on the low-carb plan.) It seems to work best when sweetening liquids, and hence my flirtation with granita, gelée (gelatin), and my favorite from the Spanish years, flan. Be aware, however, that granular Splenda in the box and Splenda in the packet are two completely different products, and the packet Splenda cannot be substituted for the granular type. A "fluffer" or extender is added to granular Splenda so that it will measure exactly equal to granulated sugar. Both types are pricey; if you plan to use a lot of it (and if you like to sweeten beverages such as tea, homemade lemonade, and cocktails, you will) it's worth searching the Internet, where substantial discounts can be found.

Fresh Figs *on* Sauternes Gelée *with* Mint Mascarpone

SERVES 4 * When I was in third grade, my friend Anne Futterman and I spent many hours debating what would happen if a person fell into a swimming pool filled with Jell-O (we never worked out quite how we'd fill it). Would you sink? Float? I've shared this quandary with many friends over the years and it always, strangely, promotes a lively discourse. Then, while attending cooking school in London, I bought 500 sheets of leaf gelatin from a catering supply store because my teacher told me it was a fantastic investment. Fifteen years later, I still had 450 sheets. Imagine my delight when gelatin dessert (now known as gelée) became fashionable, and started showing up in flavors like tomato, caviar, and Champagne! Use white bowls for maximum effect in this pretty, glittering dessert.

SAUTERNES GELÉE

3 sheets leaf gelatin, or 1 rounded teaspoon powdered gelatin (about half a packet)

1¼ cups Sauternes (sweet French wine) or orange muscat

2 sheets edible gold leaf (available in Indian and specialty markets), or 1 tablespoon finely chopped fresh mint

MINT MASCARPONE

½ cup mascarpone cheese, at room temperature

2 teaspoons granular Splenda

2 teaspoons finely chopped fresh mint

4 large, very ripe fresh figs

4 tiny, perfect sprigs of mint, for garnish

To prepare the gelée, soften the gelatin in cold water for 5 minutes (see Note). In a saucepan, combine the Sauternes and gelatin and place over medium-low heat. Stir until the gelatin has melted and the liquid is smooth and slightly viscous, 1 to 2 minutes. Remove from the heat and let cool for 5 minutes, then stir in the gold leaf until it is broken up into small, glittering pieces. Divide the gelée mixture among 4 shallow bowls and carefully transfer to the refrigerator, without sloshing. The gelée will take about an hour to set.

Just before serving, prepare the mint mascarpone by whisking together the mascarpone, Splenda, and mint in a bowl.

Slice off the stems of the figs just where the fig begins to swell. Cut each fig in quarters from the top, coming to just ¾ inch above the base, so the fig opens out like a flower. Place a large dollop of mint mascarpone in the top of each fig and carefully transfer a fig to each bowl, setting it gently atop the gelée. Garnish each plate with a sprig of mint and serve at once.

NOTE: If using leaf gelatin, fill a small measuring cup with cold water, roll up the sheets, and immerse in the water. After softening, remove the sheets and discard the water. If using powdered gelatin, place in a saucer and cover with 2 tablespoons cold water. The gelatin will swell and absorb all the water.

216 calories, 18 grams net carbs (20 grams less 2 grams fiber), 6 grams fat (4 grams saturated)

Star Anise Flan *with* Blackberries

SERVES 4 TO 6 * Flan, crème caramel, pots de crème, and crème brûlée are all variations of the basic egg custard, an amazingly versatile preparation that is also the base of the classic dessert sauce crème anglaise. Since Splenda works well for sweetening liquids, I concocted this spicy, Asian-accented flan from some aromatic star anise, spices, and citrus. It is not overly sweet, and there is no hint of bitter aftertaste to let you know an artificial sweetener is in the room (strictly speaking, Splenda is sucralose, made from cane sugar, which is not an artificial substance, but *we* know it ain't sugar). With the soothing texture of real cream, this flan is just as satisfying as the real thing and perfect for following any meal with a hint of Asian flavors.

1¹/₄ cups whole milk

²/₃ cup heavy whipping cream

4 pods star anise, or 1 tablespoon broken pieces

Grated or minced zest of 1 scrubbed orange

2 cinnamon sticks

3 large eggs

³/₄ teaspoon best-quality vanilla extract

³/₄ teaspoon orange-flower water (optional)

2 tablespoons granular Splenda

Ground nutmeg and cinnamon, for serving

1 cup fresh blackberries, wiped clean

Butter a 4-cup or similar-sized gratin or soufflé dish or individual ramekins. Preheat the oven to 325°F.

In a saucepan, combine the milk, cream, star anise, orange zest, and cinnamon sticks. Over medium-high heat, bring the mixture to just below the boiling point, then remove from the heat and let stand for 30 minutes, to infuse the flavor of the aromatics into the liquid.

Put a kettle of water on to boil for the bain-marie. In a bowl, whisk the eggs for a minute, until frothy. Then, whisking all the time, drizzle the infused milk mixture through a strainer into the eggs, discarding the solids. Stir in the vanilla, orange-flower water, and Splenda. Pour the custard into the prepared baking dish and place in a roasting pan a little larger than the dish. Pour in boiling water to come about halfway up the sides of the dish, and cover the pan with foil. Bake for 35 to 40 minutes, until the custard is set through to the center. Remove from the bain-marie and cool to warm room temperature. If desired, serve right away, or chill for up to 6 hours, covered. (Remove the custard from the refrigerator 15 minutes before serving, to awaken the flavors.) Sprinkle the top of the custard generously with nutmeg and cinnamon, and spoon the custard straight from the dish. Scatter each serving with some of the berries.

For four: 268 calories, 9 grams net carbs (11 grams less 2 grams fiber), 22 grams fat (12 grams saturated)

For six: 179 calories, 6 grams net carbs (7 grams less 1 gram fiber), 14 grams fat (8 grams saturated)

Grilled Peaches *with* Honey Ricotta

SERVES 4 * It's a little too much trouble to fire up an outdoor grill just for this dish, but it's a natural if you've used the grill to cook the main course. Or, preheat a ridged cast-iron grill pan to medium heat. The peaches should not go onto a very hot grill.

2 large, ripe peaches, washed, halved, and stoned

1 tablespoon balsamic vinegar

1/2 cup whole-milk ricotta cheese

1 tablespoon honey

1 teaspoon granular Splenda

1/8 teaspoon ground allspice

Prepare a charcoal or gas grill for medium-heat grilling, or heat a ridged cast-iron grill pan to medium hot. Place the peaches cut side down on the grilling surface and grill for about 5 minutes, or until marked by the grill and golden. Turn right side up, brush the cut sides generously with the vinegar, and grill for 3 minutes more. Transfer to a platter or individual plates and set aside. When ready to serve, whisk together the ricotta, honey, and Splenda. Mound 2 tablespoons into the center of each peach and dust the tops with a little allspice.

92 calories, 10 grams net carbs (11 grams less 1 gram fiber), 4 grams fat (3 grams saturated)

Roasted Strawberries *with* Pomegranate-Beaujolais Granita

SERVES 4 * Granitas are a versatile and simple way to create your own unique ice flavors. This version is bright, refreshing, and a deep and luminous ruby red. Roasting the strawberries concentrates their flavor, making it almost voluptuous. They do, however, end up looking a bit shriveled, so they have been buried under the craggy granita. To clean the strawberries, brush rather than wash them, or they will absorb too much water.

POMEGRANATE-BEAUJOLAIS GRANITA

1³/₄ cups Beaujolais wine

¹/₂ cup pomegranate juice (Pom)

1 tablespoon granular Splenda

12 large strawberries, brushed clean, hulled, and halved

2 teaspoons hazelnut or pistachio oil

¹/₄ cup pomegranate seeds or halved red grapes (see Note)

4 small sprigs of fresh mint, for garnish

To prepare the granita, in a large, shallow glass baking dish that will fit in your freezer, combine the wine, pomegranate juice, and Splenda. Freeze for 4 hours, stirring vigorously with a fork every 15 minutes after the first half hour, to keep the granita from freezing into a solid block. Scrape down the sides and make an even mixture of large, flaky crystals. The granita should be served as a chunky ice, not a smooth sorbet. Cover and keep frozen until ready to serve, up to 2 weeks.

About 1 hour before serving, preheat the oven to 400°F and chill 4 bowls.

Place the strawberries on a parchment-lined baking sheet and brush with the hazelnut oil. Roast for 15 minutes, until softened and caramelized. Cool to room temperature.

Divide the strawberries among the chilled bowls. Scraping toward yourself with a sturdy spoon or ice cream scoop, divide the granita among the bowls, hiding the strawberries. Scatter the pomegranate seeds over the top, garnish with the mint, and serve immediately, with large spoons.

NOTE: While the granita is freezing, fill a large bowl with water. Shallowly score the outer skin of the pomegranate into lengthwise quadrants. Peel the skin back to remove it, then break the fruit apart and place it in the water. Pull the yellow pith apart and ease out the seeds; the seeds will settle to the bottom while the bits of pith rise to the top. Retrieve the pith with a skimmer and discard. Drain the seeds and spread on a doubled layer of paper towels to dry.

150 calories, 13 grams net carbs (15 grams less 2 grams fiber), 3 grams fat (0 grams saturated)

Fresh Ginger and Mint Granita with Almond and Green Cardamom Cookies

MAKES 15 TO 20 COOKIES, SERVING 4 * This granita is based on a tea that was first served to me by the talented and soigné Hamburger-Hamlet-creator Marilyn Lewis at her pretty Westwood Village, California, restaurant The Gardens on Glendon. These unbaked cookies also make a wonderful, bright accompaniment to morning tea or coffee, and they can also be made with ground, skinned pistachios. They are a contribution from my friend and cooking partner, the award-winning cookbook author Neelam Batra.

GINGER AND MINT GRANITA

1³/₄ cups dry white wine

¹/₂ cup water

4 slices fresh ginger, about ¹/₄ inch thick (no need to peel)

1 cup loosely packed fresh mint sprigs

1 tablespoon granular Splenda

ALMOND AND GREEN CARDAMOM COOKIES

3 green cardamom pods (available at well-stocked markets)

³/₄ cup plus 1 tablespoon almond meal, ground almonds, or blanched, slivered almonds ground to a powder in a food processor

¹/₄ cup granular Splenda

2¹/₂ tablespoons instant nonfat dry milk

1¹/₂ to 2 tablespoons whole milk

Sliced, unskinned almonds, for garnish

To prepare the granita, in a saucepan, combine the wine, water, ginger, and mint. Bring the mixture to just below the simmering point, then remove from the heat and let cool completely. Strain into a large glass or ceramic baking dish that will fit in your freezer, pressing down hard on the solids. Stir in the Splenda and freeze the granita as directed on page 146.

To prepare the cookies, in a coffee grinder reserved for grinding spices or a mortar and pestle, grind the cardamom pods to a powder. Discard any large pieces that can't be ground, and measure ³/₄ teaspoon of the finely ground cardamom.

In a bowl, combine and mix together the almond meal, Splenda, instant dry milk, and ¹/₂ teaspoon of the ground cardamom. Add the whole milk a little at a time, adding just enough so that you can mix with your fingers to make a smooth—not sticky—dough.

Clean and lightly oil your hands, then shape the dough into a round ball and place between 2 large sheets of parchment or waxed paper. With a rolling pin, roll the top of the paper to flatten the dough into a 4 by 2-inch rectangle, about ¹/₃ inch thick. Remove the top piece of paper, and cut the dough into 15 to 20 pieces (either diamonds, squares, or circles—use a tiny biscuit cutter). Transfer to a serving platter, and garnish with sliced almonds and the remaining ground cardamom. Serve at room temperature. (The cookies will keep for up to 3 days in the refrigerator; return to room temperature before serving.)

Serve the granita in chilled bowls, with 3 cookies on the side.

281 calories, 9 grams net carbs (13 grams less 4 grams fiber), 16 grams fat (2 grams saturated)

Flourless Chocolate Cake
with Raspberry Sauce

SERVES 8 * Incredibly dense and fudgy, this "cake" is more like a brownie: no frills, no faux sweeteners, just glorious, satisfying chocolate. Hard to believe it clocks in at less than 15 carbs per slice.

8 ounces best-quality bittersweet chocolate, coarsely chopped

1/2 cup (4 ounces) unsalted butter, cut into 8 chunks

4 large eggs, well chilled

FRESH RASPBERRY SAUCE (OPTIONAL)

8 ounces ripe raspberries

2 tablespoons granular Splenda, or more to taste

1 tablespoon lemon juice, or more to taste

1 tablespoon Cointreau or Grand Marnier, or more to taste

Unsweetened cocoa powder, for dusting

8 fresh raspberries, for garnish

Place the oven rack in the center of the oven and preheat it to 325°F. Rub an 8-inch nonstick cake pan with butter, then place a circle of parchment paper in the base of the pan and butter the paper. Put a kettle of water on to boil for the bain-marie.

Place the chocolate in the top of a double boiler set over barely simmering water and heat, stirring occasionally, until melted and smooth. Add the butter and stir until smooth. Remove from the heat. Place the eggs in a large bowl and beat at high speed with a hand-held electric mixer for about 5 minutes, until doubled in volume. Gently fold a third of the egg foam into the chocolate mixture, until almost no streaks remain. Fold in the remaining foam in 2 batches, just until there are no more streaks.

Scoop the batter into the prepared pan and smooth the top. Place in a large roasting pan, set the pan on the rack in the oven, and add boiling water to come about halfway up the sides of the cake pan. Bake for 25 to 28 minutes, until an instant-read thermometer inserted into the center of the cake reads 150°F. The edges will be puffed but the center will look glazed and not quite done. Remove from the bain-marie and cool on a rack to room temperature. Cover and refrigerate for at least 2 hours (or overnight, or for up to 4 days). Return to room temperature before serving.

In a blender, purée the raspberries and stir in the Splenda, lemon juice, and Cointreau. Blend briefly and push through a nylon strainer to remove the little raspberry seeds. Adjust the flavor to taste with more Splenda, lemon juice, or Cointreau.

Invert the cake onto parchment paper. Peel off the parchment from the base of the cake and invert again, right side up, onto a platter. Dust the top with cocoa powder, cut into 8 wedges, and place a raspberry on each wedge. Serve with the raspberry sauce on the side.

302 calories, 16 grams net carbs (18 grams less 2 grams fiber), 26 grams fat (14 grams saturated)

Aïoli-Mayo Base

MAKES ABOUT 1¹/₄ CUPS ∗ Mayonnaise was a no-no on a low-fat diet, but followers of a low-carb regime can indulge (within reason, of course). Store-bought mayo is acceptable, but the true gourmet will want to make his or her own.

Vary the amounts of garlic and lemon juice in this eggy, smooth, and very versatile sauce, depending on how you plan to serve it.

1 to 3 large, firm cloves of garlic, thinly sliced

¹/₂ teaspoon fine sea salt

1 large egg plus 1 large egg yolk, at room temperature

1 teaspoon white wine vinegar

1 teaspoon Dijon mustard

¹/₂ cup extra virgin olive oil

¹/₂ cup canola oil

1 tablespoon fresh lemon juice, or more to taste

¹/₄ teaspoon white pepper, preferably freshly ground, or more to taste

In a mortar and pestle, pound the garlic and salt into a smooth and even paste. Scrape the mixture into a food processor (if you don't have a large mortar and pestle, push the garlic through a press into the food processor and add the salt.) Add the egg, egg yolk, vinegar, and mustard. Process until evenly blended. With the motor running, drizzle in the olive and canola oils very, very slowly at first, adding it slightly faster after the first ¹/₃ cup has been emulsified. Add the lemon juice and pepper and pulse 2 or 3 times. Taste for seasoning and add another ¹/₂ teaspoon of lemon juice and/or a pinch of pepper, if desired. (I like aïoli quite tart, especially when serving it with fish. The flavor will improve and mellow if allowed to rest for 24 hours; cover and refrigerate, then return to cool room temperature before serving. It will keep for up to 5 days in the refrigerator.)

Per 2 tablespoons: 417 calories, 1 gram net carbs (1 gram less 0 grams fiber), 46 grams fat (5 grams saturated)

Two-Week Preserved Lemons

MAKES 5 PRESERVED LEMONS ∗ Preserved lemons are a Middle Eastern staple seasoning and are found flavoring North African dishes as well. Recently adopted by the latest generation of influential chefs, this seasoning adds salty-sour complexity to any protein, and Four-Day Preserved Lemons (recipe follows) make them a little less of a project.

5 large lemons, scrubbed to remove wax, and dried

10 tablespoons coarse sea salt

Olive oil, as needed (do not use best-quality oil for this recipe)

FOUR-DAY PRESERVED LEMON ZEST

3 large lemons, scrubbed to remove wax, and dried

2 teaspoons coarse sea salt

Wash a large glass jar with abundant, very hot water and soap; rinse well and dry. Wash your hands well.

Cut each lemon into quarters, but not all the way through; leave them connected at the base like a flower. Pack 2 tablespoons of salt into the center of each lemon, then squeeze them back together and place in the jar. Squeeze the lemons down into an even layer and place a sheet of plastic wrap over the top, pressing it down so it touches the top of the lemons. Let stand in a sunny place for 1 week, pressing down on the lemons every day to compact them further. By the end of the week, the lemons will have flattened and be covered with a layer of juice; they are now ready to use. Gently pour about $1/2$ inch of olive oil over the top to keep out the oxygen, and refrigerate for at least 1 week before using. The lemons will keep for up to 6 months in the refrigerator.

When using, retrieve a lemon with clean tongs—not your fingers—and rinse well. Rinse in cold water, then trim away the remainder of the inner flesh and chop or sliver the preserved rind as needed.

VARIATION: FOUR-DAY PRESERVED LEMONS

With a vegetable peeler, remove all the lemon zest in strips; juice the lemons, and measure $2/3$ cup juice. In a small saucepan of boiling water, blanch the zest for 1 minute, then drain in a sieve. Place the zest strips in a clean, 8-ounce jar and add the salt and the juice, pressing down with the back of a spoon to submerge all the zest. Cover with a clean, tight-fitting lid and let stand at room temperature for 4 days, shaking energetically once a day. After 4 days, the zest can be refrigerated for up to 6 months. Retrieve with a fork or tongs when needed, and chop or sliver the zest as desired. Rinse thoroughly and shake off the excess water before using.

C